REMEMBERING ELI

CHELSEY TOOKEY

I would like to dedicate this book to Eli,

My beautiful Son, the one I have loved since before he existed and the one I will continue to love and miss until my last breath. My very own guardian angel.

I would like to dedicate this book also to Dean,

My husband who has literally picked me up from rock bottom time and time again, who loves and cares for me and our son, Eli unconditionally.

A message to the bereaved parents

Firstly, I want to say sorry. I am so sorry that you are having to sit here and read this. I am sorry that you find yourself in this very unfair position. I will not say "time is a healer" You will always grieve your child no matter how long it's been. The grief you feel is just all the love you have for your child. Losing your child does not get easier, every milestone and birthday you will be reminded. Every time you sit down for a family dinner, every time you see a child the same age. You will never forget about your missing child.

I will say though, that you will learn how to cope with this new reality, and it will become a new normal for you. The pain you feel now won't get smaller, but it will become easier to live with and you adapt with it. The pain is a reminder your baby existed, and it is the love you have for them. The love that you have for your child will never go away. And that is the pain you are feeling the love for your child that has nowhere to go.

You may not believe me when I say that one day you will remember how to laugh and smile again. I remember back when I would have cringed if I read those exact words, there was a time I couldn't see myself smiling, let alone laughing again. I didn't want to. But there will be a time when the good days outweigh the bad days. There will be days where you feel like you've backtracked in your grief and want to give up again, but that is ok. Even if all you get done in a day is breathe, that is ok too. I really hope that this book will help you to validate your feelings, I hope that it can help you get through the bad days you will experience, I hope it will make you feel like you are not alone and above all I hope it gives you hope.

The reason I am so open about baby loss and the experience I had when my son Eli died is mainly because I want his memory to live on. I don't want him to ever be forgotten. But also, this is me putting my pain into purpose. I hope this book helps others to get through and make you feel like you are not in this alone. I hope talking about Eli helps to prevent stillbirth happening, and to raise awareness of baby loss. If people were aware of the risks throughout the whole nine months of pregnancy then maybe less babies will have to die because of sheer lack of knowledge.

I for one did not know the risks of stillbirth. I believed that everything was fine after the first twelve weeks, but I was clearly very, very wrong. If baby loss was less of a taboo and people were more aware of it happening and spoke of it happening, then babies would not die unnecessarily.

I hope this book will help comfort you and guide you in your healing process. I want you to know that you can get through this, and I want to help you in your journey. I have included journal prompts and mindful activities in this book that I hope you will find beneficial. I want you to know that I am proud of you, I am proud of you for waking up each morning when it can feel impossible to. I am proud of you for being here reading this book and above all, I want you to know you are loved, and cared for, and you have got this. If you feel like you can't do it for yourself, do it for your babies.

CONTENTS

Eli's Story	1
Feelings	7
Preparing	27
Eli's Day	32
The Things I Wish I knew	38
Breathing After Baby Loss	43
Remembering Your Baby	52
Who Am I Now, One Year On	60
The Worst Girl Gang Ever	66
Helping to Heal Myself	70
Suffering With PTSD, Anxiety and Depression	77
Measure the Placenta	86

Helping Loved Ones Get Through Baby Loss	90
Getting Through the Holidays	101
Eli's First Birthday	110
Signs From Eli	118
Trying to Conceive After Loss	138
Dear Eli	146
Remembering Your Babies	158
Parenting Your Child in the Stars	184
Mindful Activities	188
Brain Junk	192
Journal Prompts	197
Getting Our Rainbow	228
Support For You	234

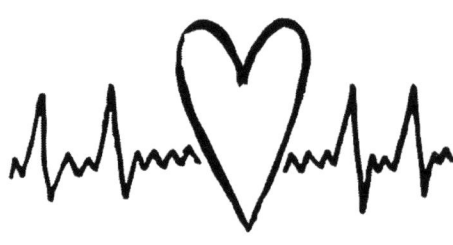

Eli's Story

Me and Eli's daddy Dean have been together for ten years and brought our first flat together five years ago. We had been engaged since we were together for two years. We have always spoke about our future, and we always wanted to be parents. We dreamed of all the places we would take our future children, the things we would do together, the traditions that would take place. We often spoke about what they would look like and be like. Dean has wanted us to have children for years, but I always insisted that I wanted to get married first. I had my plan and I wanted to stick to it. We were planning on getting married in Turkey in 2021. And then off course Covid-19 happened and mucked up everybody's plans! I became fed up and depressed as I felt like my life was on hold. We couldn't get married, and we couldn't move home like we were also planning to do. So, we decided to stop waiting, as life was evidently way too short. So that's when we decided to start our little family.

We were so lucky that we didn't have to wait for long until we had our positive pregnancy test. We couldn't believe our luck when we saw those two lines appear on the pregnancy test, we were so happy. I had never seen Dean so excited; he was ecstatic. He was in so much disbelief he made me do about five more tests! We were so excited for our future as a family of three. We started planning everything, the family holidays, the nursery, the

days out. Everywhere we went we imagined and spoke about bringing our baby with us. Ever since I met Dean, Eli had always been his favourite name. And with not much persuading it became mine too. We knew from the start, that if we were lucky enough to have a boy we'd call him Eli.

The twelve-week scan came, and it was honestly the most amazing thing. I remember holding my breath until I saw him on that screen and saw his little heart beating away. It was the most surreal, most amazing feeling. Dean was holding my hand, and both of our eyes were filled with tears. There was our little baby, my heart was bursting with pride and love for this little being on the screen. Baby Eli was such a little wriggler! I remember seeing him kicking his little legs and doing somersaults in my tummy! I had a feeling I was having a baby boy, as I was hungry all the time! I remember waking up in the night, my stomach felt so hollow where I was so hungry! I used to be up most mornings at 4am, raiding the cupboards for some cereal before I could get back to sleep. And any time I felt hungry, boy did this baby know it!! He used to kick and punch me aggressively until I ate some food. I always used to laugh when he did this, saying what a greedy baby we were going to have!

After seeing his scan pictures everyone thought he was a little girl because of his beautiful round head and long body. Every single old wives tale was also telling me I was having a girl. Off course we were all wrong, which was confirmed at an early 16-week scan. He was our perfect baby boy, Eli. We were so ecstatic. Of course all

we wanted to have was a healthy baby, but we were both desperate to have a baby boy first, so he'd be a big brother to his hopefully future little sister! As soon as we found out we were having a boy that was it, the shopping started! Nursery plans went ahead, and the furniture was brought and put up by Eli's daddy. Some would say we got rather carried away with everything we brought for him, but after the 12-week scan the baby will be fine, right?

The rest of the pregnancy went amazingly. Eli was just perfect in every way! I had a rare disease when I was a child and I also have an autoimmune disease; hypothyroidism, so Eli and I were being checked regularly to ensure we were doing fine. I had no issues during pregnancy, and I do realise how fortunate I was whilst pregnant. I didn't really have any sickness, no odd cravings, I was still managing to do light exercises and was still taking the dog out, and I worked all the way up until way past my due date. I remember being told at my 36-week scan that he was engaged and in the perfect position to give birth. We were so adamant he was going to arrive early because of this. It was in the next few weeks that followed that I was starting to feel uncomfortable where Eli was so low down. The pressure on my groin was quite severe and the heartburn I was experiencing was ridiculous. I was spending so much money on Rennie! Other than that, my pregnancy was amazing. No issues from me or baby Eli.

I had my first sweep when I was 41 weeks pregnant, and my last one when I was 41+4 weeks. That was on the 9th

December 2021 when I heard my beautiful baby's heartbeat for the very last time. The next evening, we went into the hospital after a long wait to be induced. Before they could even start the process, they were unable to detect his heartbeat. Finding out that news was the most heartbreaking and worst experience I have ever been through. It shook me to my core, and there are honestly no words to express how I felt. I didn't understand how on earth this could happen after having such an amazing pregnancy. How on earth can my baby die for absolutely no reason? They were unable to detect any abnormalities in the last final scan, other than the obvious that his heart was no longer beating. Everything looked fine apparently. Even when I gave birth to him two days later, there was still no obvious signs of how this could have happened.

11th December 2021 is the day that my baby died.

Eli was born two days later on the 13th December 2021 silent. Silent but beautiful. The love I felt for him surged from my body as I held him and watched him. My beautiful boy. He had his mamma's nose and lips, his daddy's dark, thick hair, and his daddy's ears as well. He weighed 7lb 13oz and was so tall, like his mama measuring 56 CMS! He had his mama's hands, long fingers, and long fingernails too. He was the most beautiful baby I had ever seen in my life. I was in awe of him and loved him more than I could ever have imagined.

Eli was born at 5.33am and we had two and a half precious days with our beautiful boy in the hospital. We were able to cuddle him, sing to him, read to him and just be with him. It was the best days of my life having him with us. I was so amazed by his little body, I didn't ever want to let him go. Our family were able to meet him and have cuddles with him also. Baby Eli was and still is loved so fiercely.

Having to leave him at the hospital was the hardest thing I had to do. We had to sign papers to say we gave our permission for him to have a post-mortem and we had to leave him on his own with strangers. My heart broke all over again seeing him lying there so perfectly, still and alone.

We had to wait two and a half very long months without knowing the whereabouts of Eli whilst he was having his post-mortem done and travelling to different hospitals before we were able to lay him to rest. We had the most beautiful service for him on the 22nd February 2022 where we got the chance to introduce him to our loved ones and say goodbye to him all in the same day.

After getting his post-mortem results back it turns out there were a few issues with his placenta, one being it was just too small to provide him with the oxygen he needed for the amount of time he was in my body for. His growth was so perfect throughout my pregnancy that none of the scans picked up on the placenta not being sufficient for him.

There is no footprint too small, to leave an imprint on this world.

Feelings

I have felt feelings that I didn't even know were possible until Eli died. I have felt so much anger, rage, jealousy, bitterness and so much heartache.

When we first found out Eli's heartbeat had stopped I instantly wanted him out of me, it felt so wrong him being inside of me and I begged the doctors to give me a c-section. I screamed, I cried, I begged them to tell me that they were wrong. That it was all just a big mistake. When I gave birth to him I was hoping and praying that I would hear him cry. I feel awful for saying it now, but it felt so wrong him being inside of me still when he wasn't alive.

I was in so much shock those few days at the hospital. I can honestly say I wasn't in my right mind. I asked Dean if he still wanted to call our baby Eli and I felt so guilty for even questioning it as he has always been our Eli. For weeks and weeks I punished myself for saying that, and it was only when I heard someone else say the exact same thing on a podcast where I felt at some sort of ease. Eli has had his name planned for years and years, Eli is our favourite name and I was just so sad that I wouldn't be able to shout his name out in the playground, label his clothes, and speak about him. I was wrong to think this though, I mean I won't be able to call him over or label

his belongings, but we do speak about Eli on a daily basis. Every excuse I get I say his name. All I want to do is talk about Eli, he is my son, and I am his mother so why wouldn't I want to speak about him all the time.

Every time I saw a pregnancy announcement or a post congratulating someone on their safe arrival it ate at me. I would be lying if I said it still didn't trigger me, and it can feel like being punched in the gut again and again. I felt like a failure. I felt like it was my fault and my body's fault for not saving my boy. Nobody said well done to me for giving birth to our sweet boy. Nobody asked to see photos of him or asked about my birth. It broke me, not feeling like I could talk about him and what happened. Even now when I bring up Eli's name in a conversation I can see people squirm in discomfort and try and change the subject. They don't know what to say to me in case they upset me, but people need to realise that saying nothing is so much worse. When people didn't get in touch, it made me feel like I was at fault, like I wanted this to happen. Off course it wasn't true, they just didn't want to upset me. However, Eli is on my mind 24/7. People don't realise that if they mention Eli's name it won't upset me or remind me. He's always there in my thoughts and I love nothing more than having the chance to talk about how beautiful he is and the times we had together.

In those first few weeks after giving birth to Eli, I struggled. I struggled to get through a day. I was in a zombie like state when I wasn't wailing into one of Eli's

baby grows or on the floor of his nursery. I couldn't be bothered to do anything at all, I couldn't be bothered to eat, to drink, to wash. My husband Dean really helped me in those first few weeks, and I think I became his focus. Making me better. He would prepare me food, get drinks for me, and made sure I took all of my medication. I had absolutely no motivation to do anything, I didn't even want to talk to anyone. Everything seemed to trigger me, tv shows, music I used to love. When I eventually left my house again I would find myself breaking down in public places, when I heard a baby crying or saw one go past me in their buggy. Even when I could hear toddlers calling out to their mummy's. Everything pulled at my heartstrings and reminded me of what I was missing. I even started getting upset seeing teenagers on their way to school, knowing I would never see my child in his school uniform, know what he looked like or what his personality would be like. I often look at Dean at times and wonder what Eli would have looked like and been like at his age.

Some days I didn't recognise myself, and I grew to hate myself. Not just for feeling like I failed Eli and my family, but the sheer anger and bitterness that stemmed from me. I couldn't be happy for friends, I couldn't be sad when a member of their family died who reached a significant age. I couldn't be excited for people's birthdays. I just couldn't. Eli dying shook me to my core, I felt numb to any kind of emotion of anybody else's.

Tangled up in my own grief and sadness. Too numb to feel anything else.

I had expectations for my friends and family of how they should have behaved, and how they should have supported me. A lot of the time I was met with disappointment in that. This added to my grief and sadness, and added another layer of other things I would also eventually grieve too, the loss of friendships.

A lot of them eventually stopped checking in with me. It hurt me all the time, each time another one of them let me down. It made me feel even more alone, and even more that it was my fault. When Eli first died people ignored me, walked away from me if they saw me approaching, and if I ever mention Eli I can still to this day see them squirm with awkwardness. People decided that because they didn't know what to say, they would just say nothing at all. Pretend like I was never pregnant, and Eli was just a 'blip' in my life. They thought they would remind me that my baby died if they mentioned him. But no, I can assure you Eli was not a 'blip', he is my child and I love him more and more every day. He is always on my mind, and I assure you I won't forget that my son died, something like that is etched on your memory and heart for life. Grief is all the love, that has nowhere to go. I don't mind grieving for the rest of my life, as I will continue to love Eli for the rest of my life.

I grew to hate my body, for feeling like it failed us. I grew to resent myself; it was supposed to be my baby's

safe place and it turned out to be my baby's tomb. How can one learn to love themselves again, after feeling like it's your fault your baby died. What I have learned now, is that it's not my fault. Some days I must remind myself that I did my best to ensure the health and growth of my beautiful child. I did everything I could at the time I was pregnant with him and if love could have saved Eli, he would be sitting here with me now and I wouldn't be here writing this book.

Learning to love myself again has been a challenging journey. Being reminded daily of my now changed body, brings back all kinds of different emotions. My own body was a trigger for a very long while, every time I looked in the mirror. Sometimes it still is. I have started the gruelling process of learning to love myself again, and I am learning to start looking after myself again. I grew the most beautiful human being myself, with my body, for a whole 41 weeks and 5 days. If anything, I should be so proud of myself for that.

I have started trying to be kind to myself, and stop being so resentful towards myself. I must keep telling myself that Eli wouldn't want his mum to be so unhappy all the time and that is what has kept me going. The fact that I am here today, is because of my son, I am fighting for him, and making him proud, that's all I can do for him so I will continue to try my best for him and to continue to talk about him and carry on his memory. My Eli didn't get a chance on this planet, and there are so many people are fighting to stay on this planet currently that it isn't

fair to waste my own opportunity. I am trying to enjoy life as much as I can possibly do without my boy. Being kinder to myself has been hard for me at times but I am getting better at it. If I have a griefy day I let myself have a griefy day, I don't punish myself so much anymore for having one or not having one.

Not long after Eli had first died, I would cry every single day. If I went an hour or even a whole day without crying, I would feel so guilty. Guilty that Eli might think I have moved on or that we're not sad enough that he isn't here. It took me a very long time to realise that actually Eli wouldn't like it if we were sad all of the time. That not allowing myself to try and find a bit of joy was damaging his memory. It took me a long while to realise this, and some days the grief and self-doubt caught up with me again and the whole process starts from the beginning, the guilt, the shock, the numbness. I have learnt that grief will stay with me for the rest of my life now. Learning to live after loss is so hard, and I struggled to feel like I deserve to have any joy or happiness in my life now. I have now learnt that it is ok to feel joy, that joy and grief can walk hand in hand together.

Grief is not something you can move on from, instead we learn to grow around the grief, and to carry it with us. Grief is just all the love with nowhere to go. I appreciate each day as it comes, if I'm having a particularly bad time I will allow myself to cry and feel the emotions. I have stopped trying to hide how I feel, because hiding it

away and trying to contain it just doesn't work. There was a time where I was having arguments with my brain, about how much better my family would be without me. I persuaded myself that I am a burden for them, and I should just do something stupid so they can feel joy without me here ruining it for them. It was hard getting out of this headspace, so I did what I always do and called my mum. I told her how I was feeling and how I feel like I'm letting everyone down by not letting them feel joy when I couldn't feel any, and she made me feel better. She answered the questions that my own brain was asking me which I couldn't find an answer for. The part of my brain that was telling me that I'm no good, useless, and not worthy of anyone's love and care. I was in that head space many times, sometimes it lasted a day sometimes it lasted weeks. There was a battle going on in my head constantly, and nobody but me knew about it. When I spoke to my therapist, my mum, and Dean about how I was feeling they made me feel seen, valued, and loved. They made me rationalise my own thoughts and I started disbelieving the thoughts that were going around in my head. That's when I started fighting back.

I do wonder what would have happened if I didn't speak up about my feelings, that I didn't just pretend that everything was fine all the time and tried to be "strong". I am constantly told how strong I am from other people but being strong in their opinion and being strong in my opinion are completely different things. Most people think that being *strong* is putting on a brave face for

other people. Smiling and laughing when I'm in public or on my social media. Acting like everything is fine. In my opinion though being *strong* is getting out of bed on the days you feel like you can't, for speaking up about your feelings, and for getting through another day. I hate the term "be strong" as I wish people would understand that for me, waking up every morning, getting myself up and out of bed on days when I feel like I can't that for me is being strong. The days people can't face and the days that the grief comes in waves, those are the days we are having to be the strongest. The days when I have an overwhelming feeling of guilt, dread, and pain whilst sitting at my desk alone at work, when everyone else goes quiet, and I must pull myself together and try to re-focus. That is when I am having to be the strongest, the days that to others I look like I'm the weakest.

Grief is love without a destination…

Things to do to help love and care for yourself again:

- Write three things that you are grateful for every day. This may seem so hard at first thinking of anything to be grateful for. Start off small, your first cup of coffee, the way the sun feels on your face, the love and support you have from your family, etc.

- Take a nice warm bath or have some sort of selfcare. Moisturise your face or body, wash your hair, you deserve it!

- Drink some water.

- Eat some good food and start taking vitamins.

- Go for a walk in the outdoors, feel the wind on your face, take note of your surroundings and breathe in that fresh air.

- Journal your feelings, write down how you are feeling right now. Let out any emotions you have on paper, this is what helped me process a lot of my feelings.

- If you are feeling anger or hate towards anyone write them a letter, and then burn it.

- Do something for yourself, something that you used to love doing. Whether that be a hobby such as painting, writing, reading a book, exercising. Do something that once made yourself feel good.

- Take part in mindfulness, meditation helped me for a long time. I use it to relax my brain and connect with Eli.

- Allow yourself time to cry and connect with your feelings. Crying is a good way to heal your soul. Don't be afraid to cry.

- If you are feeling self-doubt or having conflicting thoughts about yourself, print off some positive

affirmations and stick them on the mirrors around your house.

"I am more than enough".

"I let go of anxiety and self-doubt".

"I am a good mum".

- Most of all remember, don't feel bad on yourself. If you feel like you need a day in bed, have it. If you don't feel like meeting up with a loved one, say no. You must concentrate on getting through the day, getting through each minute and each hour can feel challenging and hard at times, but it is vital.

- Talk to your partner/ family about how you are feeling. Tell them what you need from them, whether it's a hug from them or an ear to listen. Or for them to make some food for you, chores that need doing, medication that needs picking up, groceries that need buying. They are your most vital support group right now, and I promise you that they want to help you.

- Write a letter to your baby, tell them how much you love them and ask them for their guidance and their strength.

-If you feel able to talk about your baby, express your emotions to a safe person who you feel like you can confide in. Talking about Eli made me feel at ease, and it was another way I was able to process what happened to him.

Things I am grateful for today:
1. *I am grateful for the sunshine on my face*
2. *I am grateful for the support from my family*
3. *I am grateful for a nice cup of coffee that I am drinking.*

Things I am grateful for today:
1.
2.
3.

Things I am grateful for today:
1.
2.
3.

Things I am grateful for today:
1.
2.
3.

Things I am grateful for today:
1.
2.
3.

Things I am grateful for today:
1.
2.
3.

Things I am grateful for today:
1.
2.
3.

Things I am grateful for today:
1.
2.
3.

Things I am grateful for today:
1.
2.
3.

Today I am feeling:
Today I am full of anger and rage. I feel hopeless and just very sad. I have cried a lot today and I am feeling grief hungover. I am going to get an early night tonight and hope that tomorrow is a better day.

Today I am feeling:
Today I have a lot of anxiety, but I slept well last night so I am feeling a bit better. I feel valued after a conversation with a friend about my baby. And I hope today will be a better day than yesterday.

Today I am feeling:

Today I am feeling:

Today I am feeling:

Today I am feeling:

Today I am feeling:

Today I am feeling:

Today I am feeling:

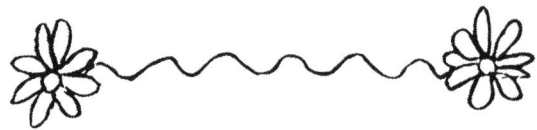

Today I am feeling:

Today I am feeling:

Today I am feeling:

Things I have done this week for myself:

1. *Went for a walk with my husband and the dogs.*

2. *Painted some memory stones for Eli.*

3. *Had a relaxing bath and face mask.*

Things I have done this week for myself:
1.
2.
3.

Things I have done this week for myself:
1.
2.
3.

Things I have done this week for myself:
1.
2.
3.

Things I have done this week for myself:
1.
2.
3.

Things I have done this week for myself:
1.
2.
3.

Things I have done this week for myself:
1.
2.
3.

Things I have done this week for myself:
1.
2.
3.

Things I have done this week for myself:
1.
2.
3.

Preparing

Nothing will prepare you to go through baby loss. I was in complete and utter shock. My pregnancy was so amazing throughout, we went to every single hospital appointment and scan, and everything was so perfect. Eli was happy and healthy. It felt like my heart was ripped out when they couldn't find his heartbeat. And the words that followed, will haunt me for the rest of my life. Baby loss is not something that is spoken about enough during pregnancy. Not once was I told my baby could die, or how many times they should be moving a day. Antenatal classes spoke all about preventing babies dying and keeping them safe after they were born, but never discussed them dying whilst still pregnant. Antenatal classes should be there to prevent your baby dying during and after pregnancy. They should be telling you how important it is to count the kicks, but unfortunately they don't, and it is something that desperately needs to change.

Since having Eli, I have spoken to other mums that are currently pregnant with their baby, and they have been told that their baby may not survive due to certain illnesses or genetic conditions. Pregnancy should be such a happy and exciting time, knowing that there is a very high possibility that you won't get to bring your baby home must be really, really hard and its something no

☆

parent should have to go through. I would have previously said I couldn't do this; however, we now know sometimes you just don't have a choice. I wanted to dedicate a chapter to the parents who are currently making their plans for their baby's birth, as well as death.

I want to tell you to make the absolute most of the time you have with your baby now, it really is the most precious time. Sing to them, read to them, talk to them. I am so pleased I did this when I was pregnant with Eli and so thankful that I did. I know Eli knows how loved he is.

I have had people ask me what they should pack in their hospital bags and I would suggest buying and packing everything you feel that you need. I get a lot of comfort from Eli's teddies that he had in the hospital with him. Knowing that my baby has touched them really means the world to me. I have kept all his clothes he wore in zip lock bags, as they still smell of him. I even have kept the top I gave birth in, also in a zip lock bag.

We were given a memory box from 4 Louis' charity, which has hand and footprint casts included which we had done. I thank them every day for providing these, as that is the only thing I got to bring home when I left the hospital without my baby in my arms. We took pictures, videos, we sung and read to him, and his grandparents did too. We were so fortunate that our families were able to meet Eli as I know that isn't always the case. We were also able to cut a lock of Eli's hair and it is currently sitting in one of his many memory boxes. It is something that I will cherish for the rest of my life as well as all the other things he touched whilst he was in the hospital.

Do what you feel is right, some people can't face meeting their baby and if that's how you feel then of course that's ok. Do not listen to what anyone else tells you to do, you need to think of you and your partner and your baby. The midwives should be very sensitive about what you want to do, if you don't feel like you can meet your baby you can always ask them to take photos for you and look at them at a later date, when you feel ready to.

Things to consider/ pack in your hospital bag:

. Do you still want to have a birth plan?

. Clothes for yourself and birthing partner.

. Clothes for your baby, we changed Eli twice whilst we were together at the hospital.

. Soft toys, anything meaningful you want to leave with your baby or have your baby hold.

. Anything personalised or personal you may want a photo of your baby with. Eli had his blanket with his name on, and I asked Dean to go and pick up his "hello world I'm Eli" vest before I gave birth to him, so he was able to wear that when he was born.

☆

. I asked Dean to bring photos from our flat too we could leave them with Eli when we had to leave him at the hospital. It was also the only way I got to have a picture with Eli and my dog together.

. Who you would like to meet your baby. Our parents and our siblings met Eli.

. Any books you want to take with you to read to your baby.

. Make sure you take your phone/camera charger with you to take photos and videos of your baby if that is something you want to do.

<u>Things I regret not having which other loss mamas were able to have:</u>

- Hand and footprint 3d castings

- Professional photos done of Eli and us at the hospital.

(There are some charity's that do this, which other parents have used. It's not something I thought about at the time for obvious reasons, but I wish I had known about this before, as Eli's photos, hand and footprints are all I have left that is physically him)

☆

I carried you for your whole life, and I will love you every second of mine.

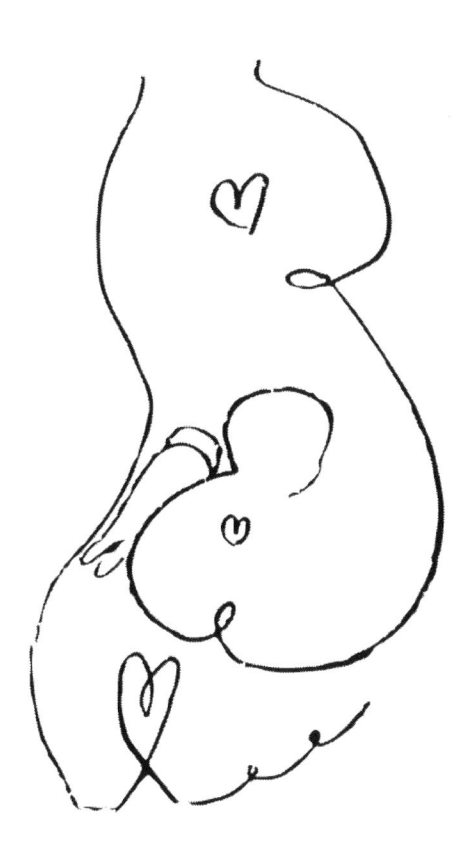

☆

Eli's Day

There is no self-help book for planning your child's funeral, so I thought I'd add a chapter about this as I know a lot of people will struggle to do this and are unsure of what to do and where to start. Some angel mamas I have spoken to since Eli died didn't have a funeral for their baby, and I know some of them regret this now. It is completely your choice if you want a funeral for your baby and I can assure you no one will judge you for what you decide on. Some people have an intimate service with their very close family and friends or can't even face the service. Whatever you decide to do please do not let anyone else cloud your judgement on what you think is best for you, your partner, and your baby.

Planning Eli's day kept me busy, and I poured all my love and pain into it. I wanted to make sure my boy had the most perfect day possible. I really focused everything I had in making sure it was perfect for him, and it did help me in keeping my brain busy, it felt like one of the only ways I could parent him. Lists were made of the things I was going to do for him, to make sure his send-off was perfect. Dean and I spent so long listening to different songs that were meaningful to us and Eli. It gave us something to focus on and it helped us grieve for our son together.

☆

I decided to give Eli a big send off. This is because I felt it was the only way I could introduce him to everyone. It was an open invitation to all of our friends and family, and he did have such a good send off. And although I was overwhelmed with the amount of people that turned up for us and him, I also felt disappointed that people I expected to go didn't turn up.

22.02.2022 was "Eli's Day" and I will continue to do something on this day every year in memory of my boy. He had the most beautiful ceremony, he really did. We asked everyone to wear something colourful, I wanted him to see a rainbow of colours. I made myself a jumper to wear with a Peter Pan quote on, I also did the same for Eli's vest, so we were matching on his special day. All of his cousins, Aunty and Nanny wore matching Lion King jumpers too. We decided on having a dove release which was so very moving and beautiful. We also had a balloon release for him. We had a photographer for his day which I thought people would find quite strange and I was slightly worried about it, but I am so, so glad I did now. Our photographer was actually booked for Eli's newborn photoshoot, so it was very special to us that she could do his day. It was nice being able to look back on those photos, I could remember hardly anything from his day as it was so emotional and painful, so having them to look back on is so special to me.

The Chaplin we had was lovely, and she gave everyone crochet hearts which Eli had with him also in his coffin. It was a nice touch and every time I go to a family members house or a friend's house and I spot the heart, it makes me feel so grateful that they have that little thing of Eli's, and it reminds me that he is so loved and still remembered. After his ceremony we had an area booked in a local pub for his wake and we had a cake made for him. He really did have the most beautiful day, and I really did do everything I wanted to do, to make sure I had no regrets about his special day.

I also felt quite silly almost for the amount of money I spent on Eli once he died, on a new outfit for him to go to sleep in and also a new blanket with his name on. I spent a fortune as I wanted to get two of everything, so I had one to keep also. I was planning on keeping the blanket to sleep with, but I am worried that I'd ruin it, so it is sitting in his memory box along with the matching Lion King outfit he was wearing on his special day. I only felt silly as I was worried about what other people would think, but like my mum said at the time, "it doesn't matter what anyone thinks, you need to do everything you want to, so you won't regret anything."

I stuck to her advice and I'm so glad that I did. I also have a couple of matching teddys, one for us and one for Eli. And both of Eli's Nanny and Grandads as well as his cousins gave him a teddy each. I made him a photo book with photos of me and Daddy, all of us at the hospital, and other photos of all our families so he knows who everyone is! We also all wrote letters for him, and I even put a lock of my hair in a teddy for him to replace the locks of hair I have of his!

Things to think of when planning your child's funeral:

- Do you want it to be an intimate service or an open invitation for all your family and friends.

- Will you be holding a wake? If so where?

- Songs you want playing at your baby's funeral. We picked three which were:

. *Lady A & Jim Brickman – "Never Alone"*

. *Kelsea Ballerini – "Peter Pan"*

. *Carrie Underwood – "See You Again"*

- What the dress code will be. We decided that we wanted everyone to be as bright as possible.

- Things you want to go in with your child in their coffin, soft toys, any letters you want to write and your family too. I took copies of everyone's letters so I could keep a copy also, I also tried to buy double of the teddys he had so I could have them as well.

- Any words or poems you would like spoken, Dean and I both said some words for Eli and we also had some poems read, including "Little Snowdrop"

- Flowers for the day. If you wish others to buy flowers for the funeral or give charity donations. I asked everyone to bring flowers as again, I wanted it to be so very colourful and beautiful for our boy. There were such beautiful flowers with teddys included on them.

- Any other things you wish to be done, for example, we had a dove release and a balloon release for Eli. I had a cake made for him at his wake also.

- If you want photos taken at your child's special day. I know a lot of angel mamas regret not having any photos of their child's special day.

- Give other people tasks to do to help. For example, my sister-in-law arranged where we were having the wake and the food. Her and my mother-in-law also oversaw getting the balloons so we could do a balloon release for him after the service.

- Choosing to cremate or bury your child is a hugely overwhelming thing to have to choose to do, something no parent should have to do. Eli was cremated and I do quite like that I have his ashes at home with me, when we go away we take him to one of his grandparents' house, so he is never alone. Some people may find it strange or morbid, but that doesn't matter to me. I love that I still have him at home with me. I enjoy spending time with his ashes, and I speak to them as if he is still here. However sometimes I do wish we had a special place for our family to visit him though, and that's why we have made a few memorial spots for Eli. If you bury your child, you need to make sure you don't want to move areas in the future. As I'd imagine it would put a future move on hold.

Little Snowdrop

The world may never notice,

If a Snowdrop doesn't bloom,

Or even pause to wonder,

If the petals fall too soon.

But every life that ever forms,

Or ever comes to be,

Touches the world in some small way,

For all eternity.

The things I wish I knew

Baby loss is a lot more common than people are aware of, as even now, it is still such a taboo subject. This is why I choose to speak about Eli as it lets other people know that they are not alone, and that all their feelings are valid. Therefore, the main thing I wish I knew is how common it is for babies to die. If more people spoke about it and it was less of a taboo subject, it could save more babies in the future.

My whole pregnancy was perfect, and Eli was healthy throughout, therefore I didn't realise that there was a possibility that he could die. If pregnant women were given more education from our healthcare system, and were made aware of all the complications that could happen during pregnancy, we would be able to advocate for ourselves and our children more and perhaps prevent so many tragedies from happening.

Off course I had heard of babies dying and of stillbirth happening, but I certainly didn't realise how common it still is. This chapter is, however, things I wish I knew after I gave birth. When I was in the 'fourth trimester',

☆

when I had no support from any one whatsoever. Just because my baby died did not mean I didn't give birth.

All I was given at the hospital was tablets to stop the milk coming in, and that was it. Once I was discharged a few days after having Eli I was basically left to it, with no advice given. No warnings of what I should expect to happen. Even though you may not have been able to take your baby home, you are still a mum, and you have still given birth.

My body is not the same as it was pre-pregnancy and I found it so hard to find anyone that I could talk to about the changes I had to my body, as I didn't want to ask anyone who had a healthy baby at home for fear of another triggering conversation! That's why I found it so helpful in finding other loss mama's. We were able to confide to each other and support each other and answer any questions we had, it made me feel so much less alone.

Firstly, you may leak milk. I was not expecting this especially as I took a tablet to dry up my milk. The first time it happened I screamed as I saw the milk dripping on my leg. I was not expecting it one bit and not knowing that it still happens is so triggering. The first period after you have given birth was horrific. I leaked through so many times, and I actually had to get Dean to go out and buy me adult nappies, as I was so heavy. Again, another trigger, but the nappies were definitely a necessity for me!

☆

Another thing I didn't realise is that your baby bump does not disappear straight away. It can take months and months for your bump to go, and I was so fearful that someone was going to ask me when I was due because I still looked pregnant. Fortunately, no one did ask this question, but that could be because I barely left the house. I felt so humiliated walking around after feeling so self-conscious of my post pregnancy body, mainly because I didn't have a baby with me to explain it. Shopping for clothes was so hard for me as my body had changed so much. Also, my stretch marks were a trigger for me. After not really having any throughout my pregnancy, the last few weeks I got loads! I was so conscious of them, but now I refer to them as my Eli stripes, and my reminder that he did exist, and he was in my belly for nine and a half months!

Your periods don't go back to normal until generally around 3 months post birth. This was really worrying for me as I convinced myself that I had turned infertile since giving birth to Eli. This is different for everyone though, so please see your GP if this is something that is worrying you.

For me going to the toilet after giving birth was one of the most painful things, I actually thought my insides were going to fall out! I was sure something was seriously wrong, and it wasn't until a few weeks after giving birth that the pains I was having went away.

☆

A lot of women lose hair after giving birth. It doesn't happen to everyone, but it does happen to the majority. It usually starts around 3 months after giving birth. A lot of women also suffer with bad body odour after giving birth, I suffered from this quite a while after I had Eli and I didn't realise this was a thing!

Of course, there are many different things that happen to every mother after giving birth as we are all different, but these are some of the things that I really wish I knew. I used to find myself googling things that were happening to me, and I was often caught off guard as the comments all included a living child as the result of the new changes to their bodies, unlike my own.

Another thing I was not expecting to experience is the different triggers there were all around me daily. On TV, on the radio, seeing pregnant women, babies, pushchairs, baby aisles in supermarkets, children, social media. Coming home to Eli's empty nursery everyday, having to put away the pushchair and the car seats that were eagerly awaiting to be filled in both mine and Dean's cars.

There was a time where everything sent me on a downward spiral, so much so that I didn't want to leave the house, I just wanted to stay inside, in my own little bubble, away from everyone and everything. Although even staying inside my home was also hard for me, being surrounded by unused baby furniture, clothes, toys all just collecting dust. It took me a long while to even

☆

be able to go into Eli's room, but some days when I couldn't sleep I found comfort in sitting in there as I felt closer to him in there.

A life may last just for a moment, but memory can make that moment last forever.

Breathing after baby loss

Eli dying was and is the worst thing that could ever have happened to me. I felt lost, alone, and empty. Honestly, I didn't want to be alive without my son in my arms. I couldn't see a future for myself without him included in it. It took me a very long time to see any hope for my future, and it was a long journey until I got there. There were many things I had to do to protect myself.

I found Social Media so upsetting at times. That was until I deleted friends and unfollowed accounts that I found triggering. Please don't be afraid to unfollow. It really does help with your sanity. Every time I saw a new baby post, it felt like my heart was being ripped out again. I tried to delete my social media apps, but I only lasted a day or so! This is because I also found social media quite helpful in my healing process, once I removed all of the setbacks. Social media was the way I expressed myself and how I keep Eli's memory alive. There were also many accounts that helped me to validate my feelings, such as other loss mums. I was able to make so many new connections with them on social media. Please dedicate some time in unfollowing all of

☆

the accounts you followed because you were pregnant, the apps you downloaded, and unsubscribe from any parenting or pregnancy emails. If you feel like you can't, ask someone else to go through it for you. I found that so difficult, receiving emails with offers for baby stuff and notifications telling me the age of my baby and the milestones he should be having.

I stopped listening to music for a while as so many different songs were hard for me to hear. Songs I used to sing and listen to when I was pregnant. Sad songs that made me feel depressed. Anything that reminded me of what I was missing. Music for Dean though was a bit of a saviour. I started listening to Podcasts about baby loss instead of listening to music. A lot of tv shows also started to upset me, and I had to stop watching a lot of the things that I used to.

I read a few baby loss books and read a lot of blogs, anything that supplied me with a bit of hope that it would get better, that the pain would ease slightly, because at the time I really didn't think it would. I started to do things that were my way in which I could parent Eli. I busied myself by creating bits for him for his memorials and his cabinet we have with all of his things in. I started collecting and painting memorial stones for him, I would then hide them whilst out in different locations. Going outside in nature is so helpful in your healing, I would always look for signs from Eli. Getting outside and going for walks really helped me mentally and physically. I always find signs from Eli when we're out, and it always validated to me that he is with us still. Journalling and writing has really helped me in my healing journey. Writing blog posts, and writing letters to Eli in my notepad.

Meditation and exercise have helped me on days when I have struggled. Finding new hobbies and interests has also helped me through. I have started hoop fitness, Dean and I started going ice skating together and now we go weekly to watch ice hockey too. Having something to focus on really helps. Doing things in Eli's memory really makes me feel at peace. We have made a little garden for him at a cemetery where he has his name plaque. We go there often and make it look lovely for him. Its really nice for us, as Eli was cremated and we didn't really have anywhere for us to go and make beautiful for him. Its so nice for the whole family to put little ornaments and cards for him. Talking to Eli when I'm indoors or on my own is my favourite thing to do. Dean and I say goodnight to him every night without fail from his bedroom window.

What I have learnt throughout my journey is to be kind to myself. To start saying "no" to things that would make me feel uncomfortable. If people didn't understand, then it was their problem, and not mine. I had to start putting myself first, to listen to my feelings and to protect my heart. When pregnancy announcements appeared, or someone told me they were pregnant, it would feel like I was being punched in the gut on repeat. When baby loss happens, the way we

☆

connect with people changes, who we once thought were our people, change. That's not our fault, it's just the way it goes unfortunately. Do what you need to do to protect your heart, if you can't celebrate a loved one's happiness then don't, if you can then by all means do. If you get invited to a baby shower, or a place where there will be children and babies, and you feel that you "should" go, but don't feel like you want to, then don't go. This is your journey, and your grieving process. Do not try to please everyone else, give yourself permission to say no. When you feel like you "should" do something, then you probably shouldn't, as it is exhausting to feel that when you haven't got the mental capability to do so.

This journey is a hard one, and we didn't choose it. Nobody would choose the journey we are on. It is so easy to suffer and make things worse for ourselves. This journey is certainly not a positive one, but it is important to ease our suffering and find some sort of growth and learning from our experiences.

After Eli died I found that a lot of my closest friends, were just not there for me as I thought they would be. I relied on them to be there for me but they just weren't. Going through baby loss has made me realise who my friends really are, and I have learnt to stop putting myself in situations where I don't want to be. I *should* go and see them, I *should* attend the event they are holding. I didn't hear much from my friends at all after Eli died, some came to see me, others didn't. As soon as they thought I was getting "better" it seemed like they wanted to see me and talk to me again. That's when I realised and said to myself if they don't want me when I'm in a bad place, then they definitely don't deserve me when I'm in a good place. It's another secondary loss in the world of baby loss, losing friends and family who you thought would be there for you and you thought would be friends for life. In a way I thank Eli for this, for showing me who my real friends are and to stop saying yes to please other people and instead putting my own needs first for once. Your people are the ones that are invested when they ask you how you are and want your honest answer, they celebrate during the high moments with you and support you through your lowest moments.

If you have your people then I am so pleased for you, we should be struggling together but also celebrating together when the time is right. We share the load and pick each other up to lighten each other's burden. That's the ultimate goal of a friendship. That is why I am so grateful I have found a community of loss mama's that are able to connect with me and understand what I am going through. There is a real sense of gratefulness talking to someone who just gets it. They understand the suffering you are going through, and you help each other get through the good times and the bad times.

Many things in life, as we know, cannot be controlled, just as the things people say cannot be controlled. For someone who has never experienced baby loss, and sometimes for those that have, they often throw words at you that they think are going to comfort you. This is one of the things I struggled with the most and I found myself in this situation so many times. When people are trying to sugar coat the situation and imply positive things can come of your child dying it makes you feel angry, hurt, and isolated. I wish I was able to move on from their words, but they would hurt me again and again, like a ton of bricks getting thrown at me on repeat, and I would repeat them over and over in my head. I used to be so upset and hurt when people would tell me how much worse it could be, or how I need to keep being positive.

It took me a while for me to realise that I wasn't the problem, and I could not see any positives about even being alive at the time. I have realised now that some people just do not like other people to show them their raw emotions, as it makes them feel uncomfortable. There seems to be such a want for people to be positive all of the time and for people not to be hurting. But the reality is that life isn't fair, its impossible to be positive and happy all of the time as that is not what life is about. So many people are hurting but don't feel like they can talk about their true feelings because they will be seen as being negative, so they shut themselves away and put on a front that everything is ok.

The positive platitudes given to us by others who think they are helping, eventually damage us even more, as all we want is for someone to listen to us and agree that life can be terrible and awful, and no one deserves to go through what we loss parents have gone through.

☆

Its so important to keep expressing your actual feelings and not putting on a front to please other people and to make them feel comfortable. I have learnt who speaks honestly and openly about feelings, and those who just ask how you are to sound polite. It is so important not to bottle up your true emotions as that's when the hate and sadness builds up, and it feels like you have no one to turn to and you end up feeling so alone. There are people out there who genuinely want to listen and want to help you, so please don't forget that.

Things to think of when setting boundaries in your life:

- Decide who your people are, those who are invested in how you feel, those who remember your baby and talk about them, those who make you feel seen and validated.

- If people no longer treat you how you feel you should be treated by them, cut ties with them.

-Communicate directly, clearly and often. It's important to let people know if they have hurt your feelings in anyway.

-Pay attention to your needs. If we are having feelings of discomfort, overwhelm or resentment it often indicates that we've allowed a boundary to be crossed.

- What activities do you find draining? If you can, stop doing them.

☆

-Focus on activities that bring you energy? Or dare I say it, joy?

-Evaluate all of your life commitments and how they make you feel, and if they are worth your time and energy.

- Learn to say "no" to people and commitments that do not serve you.

- Practise self-compassion. If you are unable to follow through with any of the above, then please try to treat yourself with kindness.

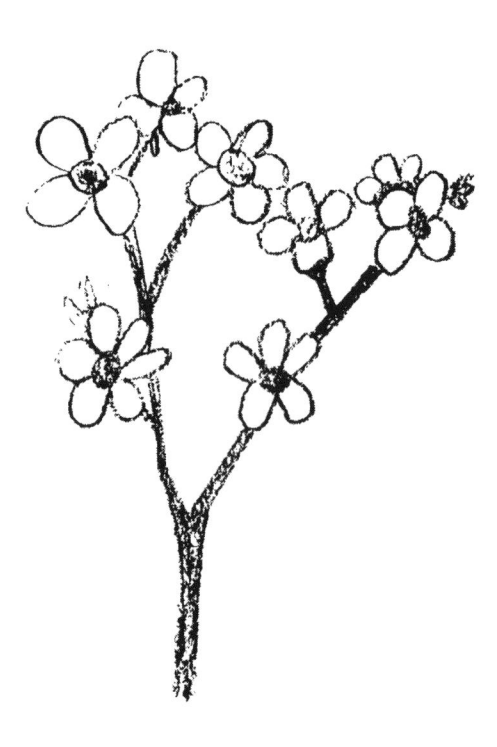

☆

Tiny footprints, oh so small,

In our hearts, you left them all.

Though you never took a breath,

You brought us love, beyond life's breadth.

In our dreams, you'll always be,

A cherished part of our family tree.

Gone too soon, but not forgotten,

You're forever loved, our little one.

☆

Remembering your baby

For a lot of loss parents, it's so important to us that our children are included, spoken about and remembered. If this is how you feel then it is so important to let your friends and families know. If you want your baby to be included in celebrations and birthdays, it's important to tell them, as so many people are under the impression that it will make us loss parents sad if they mention our babies. Off course we know this is not the case, it's not something we will ever be able to forget. For a lot of us them being mentioned fills our hearts with joy knowing they are still thought of, cared for and loved. It's so important that you articulate your feelings, wants and needs to your loved ones so they can ensure they are doing the right thing for you.

If Eli were alive he would be included in all of our family celebrations, he's still mine and Dean's child so of course we still want him to be included in celebrations and to be celebrated on his birthday. If anything, it just ensures that no one will forget him, as ultimately that is our worst fear. I will always sign cards with Eli's name

☆

on, I have also just ordered myself his hand and footprint on a stamp so I can still include his prints in everything.

'Eli's garden' is a very special place where we and other family members can visit. Arriving there seeing that Eli has been gifted new ornaments and toys is the best feeling. Also, he has other memorial plaques scattered around, Eli's bench is situated in Nonsuch Park in Surrey. One of our favourite local parks where we went regularly to walk the dog, whilst Eli was still safe in my tummy.

I will be celebrating his birthday each year with my family. I might even try and make him a birthday cake! Eli's day was the 22nd February 2022, and I would like to organise some sort of charity walk for him each year, where we do a balloon release. I have so many ideas of what I would like to do, to celebrate our Son.

Me and Eli's daddy decided to get married six months after Eli died. It was my need to focus on something, and to keep my brain busy. We made sure we included Eli in our special day though in many ways. We had silk flowers saved from his special day which went in my bouquet, along with a charm where I had his picture hanging from my bouquet so he essentially walked down the aisle with me. Our nephew was our page boy and he carried Eli's aching arms bear down the aisle with him. We had another dove release for him from the same company that had done the dove release on Eli's day. We had his easel up which we had made for his special day, we included him in our cake topper and we had a frame made for all of the people missing in our lives. He was spoken about in each speech which was so lovely to hear, I always love it when my son's name is mentioned.

As I said before it is so important to inform your loved ones if you want your child included. I made sure I took the time to tell all of my loved ones that I always want Eli to be included in our family as he is our son. Whether that be his name included on Christmas cards, him to be spoken about, and celebrated at his birthday and at other special occasions.

There are many different ways in which you can remember your precious babies. Things that seem little to others but mean the absolute world to us loss parents. Writing your child's name anywhere in nature, with rocks or in sand for example. Including them in special occasions, by having a photo of them up in the spot they should be sitting with a candle lit for them. Having a special shelf full of their memorial items, or things that have been gifted to you from other people for your baby, somewhere you could add to over the years when you see something new that reminds you of your baby. A special Christmas tree for them filled with their special ornaments. This could be a nice way to remember them over Christmas, and you could buy or make a new ornament for them each Christmas. You could include your baby's name in any cards or letters you write.

☆

When I include Eli and do something for him, I feel like its my way of parenting him, and my way of connecting to him. I find it so wholesome when I do things for him.

Things you could do to remember your baby:

- Create a memory box: Gather items that remind you of your baby, such as ultrasound pictures, hospital wristbands, baby clothes, or special keepsakes. Place them in a special box or container and revisit it whenever you feel the need to connect with your baby's memory.

- Talk about your baby to your partner, a family member, or a friend.

- Write a letter to your baby: Express your feelings and thoughts by writing a letter. You can share your hopes, dreams, and the love you have for your baby. You can tell anything you want to. How much you are missing them, how you are feeling or events that have taken place or any plans you may have.

- Make a journal for your baby: Include any drawings or words that express the love you have for them. You could include poems and photos.

- Plant a memorial garden or tree: Create a dedicated space in your garden or plant a tree in memory of your baby. You can choose flowers, plants, or ornaments that hold special meaning to you. Spend time in this space as a way to reflect and honour your baby's memory.

☆

- There are lots of different dedicated baby memorials around the UK, for example ones made by SANDS baby loss charities and your local cemetery may also have a dedication children's memorial garden.

- Engage in creative expression: Find a creative outlet that allows you to express your emotions and honour your baby. This could involve painting, drawing, writing poetry, or creating music. Use art to remember and celebrate your baby's life. You could make or paint something for them.

- Light a candle: Set up a special area in your home where you can light a candle in remembrance of your baby. You can do this on significant dates, anniversaries, or whenever you feel the need to connect with their memory. Allow the candle to burn as a symbol of their presence.

- Support a charitable cause: Consider supporting a baby loss charity or organization in honour of your baby. This could involve fundraising, volunteering, or participating in events that raise awareness and support for families who have experienced similar loss.

- Create a memorial piece: Design a personalised piece of jewellery, artwork, or other memorial item that symbolise your baby. This can serve as a tangible reminder of their presence in your life.

☆

- When you are out next write your child's name somewhere, write it in the sand, or write it on a tree, anywhere you can think of.

- Listen to a song that reminds you of your baby.

- Watch a film that reminds you of your baby.

- Meditate whilst connecting to your child.

-Talk to your baby out loud, read them a story, tell them about your day.

- Share your story: Sharing your experience with trusted friends, family, or support groups can be a meaningful way to remember your baby. Speaking about your baby and their impact on your life can help keep their memory alive and provide support to others who have gone through similar experience.

- Make a photo album or scrapbook with all the photos you have of your child if you have any, and any pregnancy photos you have. I have scrapbooks filled with my memories with Eli, I also like to put in any signs I receive from Eli.

- Keep a folder with any certificates you may have collected from charity events in your baby's memory. I adopted a lion in Eli's name, and I have that certificate in his folder too.

☆

Ideas of what you can put in your child's memory box:

- Photos including ultrasounds of your baby.

- Jewellery and trinkets that make you think of them.

- Keepsakes you have of them such as pregnancy tests, handprints, locks of hair, hand moulds, voice recordings, heartbeat recordings, their favourite items, hospital wrist bands, and any pieces of clothing you have of theirs.

- Any cards you have of theirs such as sympathy cards, birthday cards, baby shower cards, cards from their funeral flowers.

- Flowers pressed from their funeral.

- Pictures and letters to your baby.

- Mementos from memorial events.

- Any clothes that you may have had for them which are special to you

- Any fundraising certificates you may receive in memory of your baby.

- Any signs you receive from your baby such as white feathers, and things that make you think of them.

Empty cradle, broken heart,
Reaching out for him in the dark,
Bereaved mother with empty arms.
Silent sorrow, hidden tears,
Endless questions, unspoken fears,
Precious child, I miss you so,
But in my heart, I'll always know.

☆

Who am I now?

One year on

One year on and it feels like it's taken me forever to get into my current headspace. If I read these words a few months back I would have raged at it. I could never have imagined I'd still even be here; I didn't want to be. But despite everything here I am, one whole year later and I am so proud of myself. Don't get me wrong, there are still days that feel like I am just weeks into my grief again, but other days are filled with some joy now.

Time hasn't made this easier, I have learnt how to accept my grief, and I have adapted as a person because of it. One thing I have learnt since Eli died is that he is still here, not in human form but spiritually he is. There is nothing I want more, than to be able to see, hear and feel my son, but I know that it is impossible. As much as I wish I didn't have to do this life without Eli, I know I have no other choice. This was the life I was given, and if Eli doesn't get to live, I will make sure I try and live my life to the fullest for Eli and for all the other children and people that are fighting for their own lives, to be on this planet.

☆

I see and feel Eli in everything I do. I can feel him around me all the time. He keeps me going, and I just know he listens to me when I speak to him. He has given me an unbelievable number of signs that he is around still, and I am so grateful to him for that. He has made me the woman I am today, if it wasn't for Eli I wouldn't be this strong woman that I am now. He has given me a fire in my soul, which I didn't dream was possible. He has made me want to fight for him and protect his memory.

I never thought I would be able to survive my child dying, but I have and here I am a year later and still doing life. Still showing up, and although some days I can't think of anything worse. I do it, I do it for Eli. I'm sure that when Eli died, he gave me a part of his soul. Sometimes I don't recognise the woman I have become, and there have been times that I have hated myself for it. The girl I used to be could never survive this, and a part of me died with Eli. But the part Eli left me made me a fighter, it kept me going and I will forever be grateful to Eli for that. I am here today, because of Eli. Because every time I couldn't face the day, or I felt the consuming number of emotions and grief, I asked him to give me strength. And he does, every time I ask for it, he gives me the strength to keep going.

I hate that this is now my life, but I would never, ever swap it for anybody else's life. I would do it all again to make sure I had Eli in my life still, because I am eternally grateful for him. I am so proud of Eli, and proud that I am his mum. He has given me a new appreciation of life. Before Eli I used to be so wrapped up in getting things done and ticked off my to do list, I stressed about making sure I got all my work done, and just minor life things. Now I have a new outlook on life, I take notice of the little things now. I go outside and feel the air on my skin, I am always on the lookout for signs from Eli, I watch the animals, I look at the sky, watch the rain and just appreciate all the nature that surrounds me. I look at the moon and the stars each night. I really appreciate all these amazing things, that I didn't even take notice of before. It's like my eyes have reopened to the world that I live in and it's not always about doing mundane tasks that need to be done. I have started doing different things that I enjoy doing, that I couldn't find the time to do before such as painting and writing. Life should be about living, enjoying yourself, making yourself feel good and spending time with your loved ones and making precious memories, whilst you are still able to.

Some days I wake up and I cannot physically believe that this is now my life. I don't want to believe it. Days when I feel like that, I let myself feel those feelings, I sit with it and hope tomorrow is a better day. I wish I could say that it gets better, and time is a healer but we all know that I would be lying. Time does not heal us; we grow with our grief, and we learn to cope with it better after time. It's always there though, always waiting to creep up on us again. I have come to the realisation that I

☆

do not mind that I will be grieving Eli for the rest of my life. Grief I've learnt, is just love with nowhere to go. So, I sit with my grief, and I embrace it, for if there was no grief there would be no love, and I will love Eli for the rest of my life because he's my child and that's what us mums do.

It's taken me a while to get to the place where I am now, I still have days where the guilt creeps in and I blame myself that Eli isn't here. I must remind myself that it simply isn't true. I am so proud of myself that I made it, there were so many days where I was wishing I wouldn't wake up and I could be reunited with Eli forever. I am so glad and proud that I didn't listen to the demons that were in my head, and now I make sure I live the way Eli would have wanted me to live. I just want to make him proud of his mum. I will never be "healed" from the death of my child, I will carry the grief every day for the rest of my life, but I'm ok with that. The grief I have for Eli is the love I have for him, and that will never ever leave me.

I've given myself time to grieve, I've taken steps to help myself and my mental health, like going to therapy weekly, giving myself space to feel my feelings, to cry if I need to, to talk to my loved ones, and little things like walking the dog, getting out in the fresh air, eating healthy, meditating, and exercising. I am so proud of how far I have come, being kind to yourself is a necessity as hard as it can be sometimes. Using positive affirmations can help with this if it feels impossible at the time.

I remember not long after Eli died when I was reading baby loss books and I couldn't imagine myself being where they were, feeling any joy whatsoever and feeling like the world has ended. It used to really infuriate me when they spoke about life after loss, and you can feel happy again. I have proven myself wrong though, just as you can. There are days where I feel so much gratitude and joy, of course there are days where I feel nothing but sadness and anger, but I let myself feel those feelings, I cry it out and try again later in the day or sleep it off. I promise you, one day it is possible to feel joy and happiness again.

You will get there; you just have to keep on going and believing in yourself.

☆

In the blink of an eye, you were gone,

Leaving us here to mourn and long.

Your time with us was much too brief,

Yet you filled our hearts with love and grief.

You'll always be our precious one,

Shining brightly, like the moon and sun.

We hold you in our thoughts and dreams,

Forever cherished, in silent streams.

The worst girl gang ever

When Eli died I thought I was the only person to have gone through this. Babies dying is not spoke of a lot, and I really thought I was the only person in the world. I couldn't understand why I was the one who's baby died, I still of course don't know that answer but I do know that I am not alone. There are a lot of people that are also wearing my shoes. When Eli died I made an Instagram account for him @remembering.eli and I have been able to connect with so many other mama's going through the exact same pain as I am. Being an angel mama really is the worst thing in the world, and we are legit in the worst 'girl gang' possible. But the women who are in this horrible girl gang, as we call it, I can honestly say are the kindest people I have ever known. The only people I spoke to that truly understood how I was feeling and mirrored my feelings and emotions.

Why me? That was always the question, why me? Why Eli? What did we do to deserve this? But then when I started connecting with other bereaved parents, I realised it's so much more common than people are led to believe, so then my next question was why not me?

☆

Babies die every single day, and because it is still such a taboo subject nobody speaks about it enough. Miscarriage is the most common kind of pregnancy loss, affecting around one in four pregnancies*. So why wouldn't it be me in that statistic too?

*https://www.miscarriageassociation.org.uk/information/miscarriage/

This journey is so hard, and it can feel so lonely. But please know that you are never alone, there are so many of us going through the same or a similar experience. If you type in #babyloss on Socials, you will find so many brave and brilliant women and men talking about their journey and remembering our children. The women I have met throughout my journey, have been the most supportive people. Although no experience is the same, the fact that these women understood how I was feeling brought me so much comfort. I finally felt heard and understood. So many of us feel the same feelings, and have the same thoughts, it was then I realised I wasn't alone, and I didn't feel so lonely. They weren't trying to give me positive platitudes to make me feel "better", as they knew positivity wouldn't heal me, in fact they knew it would make me hurt more, angered more, and bitter more. Someone agreeing with the pain and hurt you are feeling, makes you feel validated, and above all normal.

One angel mama, Sarah reached out to me a week or so after Eli died. Her baby is named Theodore and he died a few days before Eli. I have spoken to her every single day since that first message. She lives quite far from me, but we have managed to meet in person a few times. I

☆

can honestly say we have saved each other, on many occasions. We've been there for each other throughout our sleepless nights, and we always reach out to each other if we are having a bad day. She has honestly been my rock throughout all of this, and we always say that we're sure our boys brought us together and that wherever they are, we know they are together and are besties.

Reaching out to other loss mama's is honestly a life saver, it really is. Having someone to talk to who gets it, someone to confide to who understands your pain, it really did make me feel validated and so much less lonely.

I really do have so much to thank Sarah for, for talking to me and listening to me. For knowing what to say and do to help me get through the awful days, where I felt like the weight of the world was dragging me under and when I was at rock bottom and could see no way out.

If I could encourage you to do one thing, it would be to reach out to others that have been through the same or a similar experience to you. Talking to others who have also experienced child loss is the one thing that helped with my healing. Talking to other people that have experienced 'real' grief. Grief is such a taboo thing to talk about for some people because they believe being negative will not help our 'situation' and that we need to be positive in order to heal. People that have experienced what I call 'real' grief will know that none of the above is true. That the importance of speaking about your true feelings and thoughts is the only way to be able to grieve and in time perhaps heal. I say heal; your child dying is not something that you can physically heal from. But it enables you to process your trauma and validate what you are feeling. Grieving and the trauma that comes with it is so exhausting. It is physically and mentally draining and being force fed positive platitudes and 'at leasts' is detrimental to our mental health and our grieving process.

Even when loved ones depart, they continue to accompany us in every moment and memory.

☆

Helping to heal myself.

(When no one else could)

I can honestly say that getting through my baby dying has been the absolute worst experience of my life. There are days I feel hopeless and alone. There were and are still so many days when I wake up and I just don't want to be here anymore. Sometimes I can't physically see myself in this world without my beautiful Son, I can't imagine life going on without him. However, one thing I have learnt through all of this is how painful it is to lose your child. And so, I could not put my mum, my dad, or my husband through losing me as well.

So, every day I have battled on for them. For the people that love me, because a lot of people love me, even on days when it feels like the world is against me and people stopped caring and loving me and I must remind myself that they do care still and they do love me, and they don't see me as a burden. I must go on for them, but mainly for Eli who is my reason. I must go on for him, I must be his eyes and ears and live for him as well as for me. Eli didn't get the chance to live his life, so I must live my life for him. If I gave up it would be insulting to

☆

him and his memory. He fought so much to be here, so I am now here fighting to be here for my little boy. To make him proud of his mummy.

As long as I can remember I have always been a 'busy' person. As in, most of the time I just can't sit still. When Eli died, I coped the same way very much. Constantly busying myself and not giving myself time to think, as I know as soon as I started thinking that's when the breakdowns would come, and the feelings of hopelessness and loneliness would emerge. I busied myself constantly, whether it was something to do in memory of Eli, making things for him, writing to him or about him, everything I did in honour of him, was a happy distraction for me.

I brought myself a notebook and every time I feel sad, and I am just missing Eli, I write to him in the notebook. It really helps me to feel more connected to him. I meditate to get myself to sleep, but mainly so I can speak to Eli in my head. I have lots of conversations with him in my head at night, and I picture how he would look now. I ask him to touch my face and call me crazy, but I can feel his little hands on me. I also meditate throughout the day, holding on to his teddy bear and his crystals I got for him and myself before his special day.

I have been making scrapbooks with all my pregnancy photos and have written down all my special memories I have with Eli in my tummy. All the things he used to go crazy for when in my tummy such as foods, etc.

☆

Doing different things in Eli's memory also makes me feel so much better. Whether I write his name in the sand at the beach, or I write his name on a rock. Little things I do for him, make me feel so much better. It's the only way I can parent him by keeping his memory alive, so that's what I love to do.

I started painting memory stones for Eli and placing them in different locations. My Dad and brother even took some to South Africa to place for me. I love knowing that my baby's name is everywhere! I also started planting flowers for Eli and he has several different memorial areas located in various family members gardens.

Mine and Dean's wedding was definitely a big distraction for me and helped me to busy myself through the pain of losing Eli. I loved thinking up different ways in which I could include Eli in our wedding and spent a lot of time planning and distracting myself from my pain.

Talking is a huge healer. It is so important to talk to your loved ones about how you are feeling. I know a lot of people struggle with this part, however I do make a constant effort to check in on my own feelings, as well as my partners and other family members. It's good to speak up about how you are feeling whether that's to family, friends, or internet strangers who have become my biggest supporters and my best friends!

Writing about how I feel really helps me to focus. I made a blog at the beginning of my grieving journey, to just write about my feelings and thoughts. When I feel the anger and emotions build up in my head, and I can't focus on anything else, I sit, and I write. I write and write until my head feels clearer and I feel like I can breathe again afterwards.

It's so important that you offer yourself compassion. You have been through so much and you are already feeling awful about all what has happened. There is no point criticising yourself, as hard as it can seem sometimes. I understand that this can be so much easier said than done, me being the world's worst self-criticiser. However, I am learning how to do this and I'm being kinder to myself every day. It is so vital to be kinder to yourself when you're already suffering with so much already. Just look at how far you've come already, and sitting here reading this book is a step you are taking for yourself, so you should be so proud.

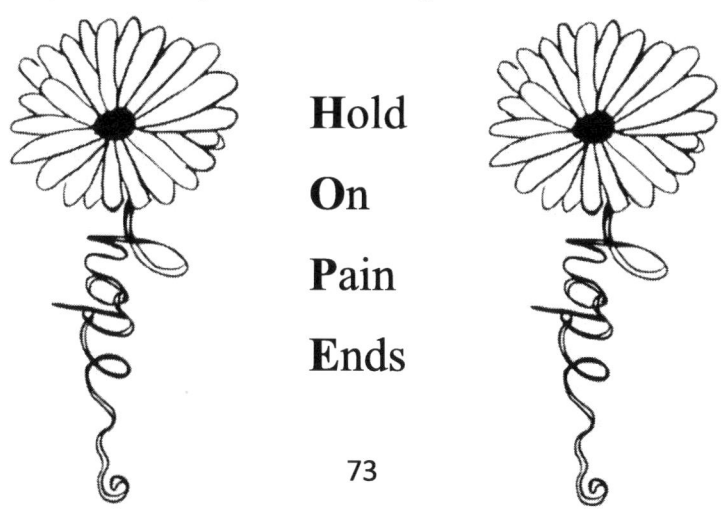

Hold

On

Pain

Ends

☆

Things you can do to help with your own healing.

- Reach out to loved ones: Share your feelings with family members and close friends who can offer emotional support and understanding. Sometimes, simply talking about your emotions and memories can be so helpful.

- Support groups: Consider joining a support group specifically for parents who have experienced baby loss. These groups provide a safe space to connect with others who have gone through similar situations and can offer empathy and guidance.

- Professional counselling: Seek out a therapist or counsellor experienced in grief and loss. They can provide a supportive environment to process your emotions and develop coping strategies.

- Online communities: Connect with online communities dedicated to baby loss support. There are forums, social media groups, and websites where you can share your experiences, find comfort, and receive advice from others who have been through similar situations.

- Non-profit organisations: There are organisations that specialize in providing support for parents who have experienced the loss of a baby. These organisations often offer counselling services, support groups, and educational resources.

- Memorialisation: Consider creating a special memorial or remembrance for your baby. This could involve

☆

planting a tree, creating a memory box, or participating in events or ceremonies that honour your baby's memory.

-Be kind to yourself: What would you say and how would you act towards someone else who was suffering like this? What would you tell them?

-Every time you have a bad thought about yourself, or your experience write it down, and then write what advice you would give someone else if they said it.

"It's my fault my baby died".

"It's not your fault, you had no control over your baby dying, you did absolutely everything you could to ensure your baby was happy and healthy. You grew him and loved him unconditionally. You did that so well".

Every time you have one of these bad thoughts you can go back to your notes and tell yourself what you would tell someone else going through a similar experience. It can help if you tell yourself these things out loud a few times, looking at yourself in the mirror. Say it with power and tell yourself that you're amazing.

-Be understanding to yourself and speak kindly towards yourself, for example when I was suffering with PTSD, I would tell myself.

"It's no wonder you're feeling frightened because you have just had unwanted memories of the past. You are safe now".

☆

- If you are having bad thoughts about yourself, you could print off some positive affirmations for yourself and read a few of them out loud to yourself in the mirror.

"I believe in you".

"I am so proud of you".

"I am enough".

"I can do hard things".

"I am the best mummy to my child/children".

A soul too brief, but deeply loved, sent to us from heaven above. You brought us joy, though you couldn't stay. In our hearts, you'll always stay.

Suffering with PTSD, Anxiety & Depression

Since Eli died I have suffered immensely, I have post-traumatic stress disorder, anxiety, and depression. I have had a few counsellors now and therapists also. It's important that you choose the right one for you, and you feel like they are helping you. There are so many out there that aren't always the right ones for you.

I received CBT therapy, and it was so beneficial to my wellbeing. My therapist Julia helped me understand that I was not to blame for the death of Eli. She helped me to realise that the emotions I was feeling, were completely normal. I spent so long feeling like I was going insane. We did several different things to help my recovery, focusing mainly on my PTSD. I was experiencing flashbacks, reoccurring smells, nightmares, panic sweats, amongst other things. She taught me different grounding techniques, we spent many sessions reliving my experience, and she taught me how the brain works and why I was experiencing the things I was experiencing.

My brain did not process the trauma of what I had been through at the time it happened. It was in a state of shock and denial. My therapist taught me that because of this the trauma my brain had not stored the memories where

☆

normal memories are stored in (the hippocampus part of the brain). They were in the amygdale part of the brain.

I learned that the amygdala, is part of our 'threat system' and its job is to keep us safe by alerting us to danger. It does this by setting off an alarm in our body, by triggering the 'fight' or 'flight' response, it gets us ready to act. When the 'threat' system is active, the hippocampus doesn't work so well. It can forget to tag the memories with time and place information, which means they sometimes get stored in the wrong place and feel as if they are happening again, right now. These flashbacks of memories can come back to us without any warning at all, when you're out shopping, driving, at work, or through nightmares. And your body is triggered into 'fight' or 'flight' mode. Once this happens it's hard to ground yourself back to the present moment, but there are a few different techniques that can help with this.

My therapist Julia described our brains as being like linen cupboards. In the hippocampus part of the brain, all our memories are stored nice and neatly away, in chronological order ready to be taken out and looked at when I wish too. However, because I had not processed the events that had happened to me previously, they were a mess, all cramming out of the linen cupboard and random memories would push themselves out of the closed door, and that's when I would experience flashbacks when I least expected it.

☆

Once I understood why I was having flashbacks, we spent our weekly sessions reliving the experiences that were giving me flashbacks. I shut my eyes, and went through exactly what happened, as if it were happening again. I described what I could see, what I was feeling, what I could smell. We finished the session when I felt like I was in a safe space. It was so hard for me, and it was so emotionally draining. I would then have to rewatch the videos and between us, we picked out all the trigger points in the video.

The reason Eli died, how it was all my fault, how I was a bad mum, how I was treated during and after pregnancy and many other things. We then went over those trigger points together, with new memories. Such as the reason why he died, and how it wasn't my fault, how I am a good mum, etc.

After we had picked out the points of my story that caused me the most distress and added new memories to them, we would then go over reliving the experience again, with the new memories added. I then had to rewatch the video of me going through the memory again and again, until my anxiety levels reduced when I rewatched it. It wasn't easy, and I wouldn't pretend it was, but it helped a lot. I do still suffer sometimes with PTSD and flashbacks, but they have reduced significantly, and I have learned different grounding techniques now which help me refocus and shift my attention from the tightness in my chest. I learned many different grounding techniques during therapy which I will list at the end of this chapter, as it may be beneficial to you and your recovery.

After we went through the memory reliving, we spoke about things I wanted to improve on, or be able to do again and set tasks together on how I could help myself to achieve these things, and what was stopping me. We set tasks to improve the things that were still triggering to me, such as seeing other friends and family's babies that were a similar age to Eli.

One of my tasks was to meet up with my cousin and her baby at a park, and just be able to look at her baby as it was something I hadn't been able to do since Eli died. I even shocked myself when I was able to not only look at him, but I even had a few moments where I spoke to him, held his hand, put his dummy back in his mouth, etc. I realised that it was my brain stopping me from doing certain things, and the worry that I would have a meltdown and be an emotional wreck. It made me realise that it was all in my head, and she helped me to realise that I didn't have to be scared or unsure of doing these things, and it was my brain stopping me from wanting to do these different things by giving me fear.

It's important to remind yourself that you are safe if you are experiencing any unwanted memories or flashbacks. There are many ways in which you can do this such as:

Proof- Carry something that proves you survived, e.g. a photo of something good that has happened since your trauma(s).

☆

Letter- Write yourself a letter reminding yourself that you are safe now and carry it with you.

Coping statements- "I survived", "This is just a memory", "This too shall pass", "I am safe now".

Then Vs Now- Focus on what's different now compared to the time of your trauma.

Different Grounding Techniques.

Come back to your senses.

5, 4, 3, 2, 1 technique

5 things you can see, 4 things you can hear, 3 things that you can touch, 2 things that you can smell, and 1 thing that you can take.

If this is too overwhelming for you to do, you could keep it simpler with just concentrating on three things you can smell, for example.

You could also do other things to bring you back to the present such as splashing your face with cold water or having a bath or shower. You could smell a strong smell such as coffee, or a candle. You could eat something with a strong taste such as a mint. You could also have a grounding object with pleasing sensory properties such as a pebble, a beaded bracelet or I sometimes keep a crystal in my pocket.

☆

Personally, I found the touch sense to be most beneficial to me, so I started putting cream on my hands and massaging them if I was triggered. I also found having sweets or mints would help when I was out in public and I was triggered, and I would focus on what I could taste. If I didn't have any mints or anything on me, I would focus on looking around. at different things I could see, and hear etc.

Use your body.

Using your body can help you to come back to the present moment if you are feeling distressed.

Change position, from sitting to standing for example.

Exercise, go for a walk or a run, or do some star jumps.

Stretch out your body, reach up and try to touch the sky with your fingertips and then bend down to touch your toes.

Dance, put an upbeat song on and dance around your living room!

Ground yourself, press your feet into the floor and literally 'ground' yourself. If you could do this barefoot on the grass even better.

Curl your fingers or toes and then release them, do this a few times.

☆

Distract yourself.

Using distraction can help bring you back to the present if your mind keeps going to unhelpful places.

Being outside in nature is one of the best therapies in my opinion. Go for a walk, feel the wind on your face, watch the clouds, the trees, and the birds. Lookout for signs from your baby.

Things to do to help to distract yourself:

-Phone or message someone who loves and supports you

-Go to a different location where you can people watch. *Be mindful where you go, you may not want to go somewhere where there will be other people's babies or children present.

-Watch a funny video, or something that makes you feel safe.

-Read a book.

-Listen to a podcast, or music that will help lift your mood.

-You could also walk somewhere slowly and mindfully, concentrating on each step you take.

Calm yourself physically.

Breathing

Try a relaxed breathing exercise to calm yourself by slowing and deepening your breathing. There are lots of meditation sounds and videos you could use to help with a guided meditation. I often use them to fall asleep with, otherwise I sometimes cannot sleep due to my mind racing constantly.

Muscles

Try a progressive muscle relaxation exercise to calm yourself and release tension. Clench and release your fists, allowing tension to drain away as you release. There are a lot of different exercise videos available online which are believed to help people with trauma, such as rocking exercises.

You could also do a few things to calm yourself physically such as exercise, yoga, stretching and also connecting with someone else, or an animal. Hugging someone or petting an animal is known to release a hormone called oxytocin which can induce anti-stress-like effects such as a reduction of blood pressure and cortisol levels. Oxytocin is also referred to as one of our "happy hormones".

Born on earth,

to bloom in heaven.

Measure the placenta

The main reason Eli died was due to his placenta being too small to meet his needs. If we were able to detect problems with the placenta in pregnancy, then babies' lives could be saved, including Eli's. The placenta is the organ that keeps the baby alive, but despite this it is not currently routinely measured in the UK.

Measuring the placenta could ensure it is big enough to provide the baby with the nutrients and oxygen needed to survive. In a routine scan appointment, parts of the baby's body (head, tummy, leg) are measured to check how it is growing but the placenta is not measured even though it keeps your baby alive for the nine plus months that they are in your womb. This is not because it is difficult, measuring the placenta can be easily done by ultrasound scans and we already have the equipment available to us. It takes roughly thirty seconds to measure the placenta, so why on earth is it not already a compulsory check to be made by our healthcare providers?

☆

The placenta is the most vital organ that provides life to babies whilst they are growing in the womb. The organ that is the baby's lifeline. You would think that the placenta would be checked to ensure the measurements of it are in proportion to fit the baby's needs. As parents we are putting our own safety and wellbeing as well as our unborn children in the care of healthcare professionals, we would assume that vital checks like measuring the placenta are carried out and we wouldn't have to ask them to do it.

If Eli's placenta was measured in a routine ultrasound scan when I was pregnant, the problem could have been identified meaning he would be here alive and well today. I would have needed to have had him earlier than I did. I was 41 weeks and 5 days pregnant him when his placenta stopped providing him with oxygen and led to his death.

It is so simple and easy to measure the placenta. There are different ways that it can be done while a fetus is in utero to estimate the size of its placenta. One way requires 3 measurements (width, height, and thickness) that can be entered into a formula to determine the volume of a placenta in cubic centimetres, using a free app called Merwin's EVP Calculator.

At the moment, placental measurement at 23 weeks' of pregnancy is routinely performed in the Rainbow clinics in Manchester. Rainbow clinics are specifically for parents who have previously experienced the devastating loss of a baby. The rainbow clinics have researched the role of measuring the placenta, and the blood flow to and from the placenta and found that this information is helpful in working out how likely mothers are to have problems with baby's growth later on in pregnancy. Although this test is used in Rainbow Clinics, it is my belief that this should be routine to prevent people having to experience the death of a baby in the first place.

I have since been in touch with Professor Alex Heazell at Tommy's Rainbow Clinic who confirmed that if Eli's placenta was measured at 23 weeks gestation it would likely have shown up small and then I would have had more surveillance, which may have detected problems and I would have had to have him earlier than 41.5 weeks, meaning he would still be alive today. Professor Heazell believes that placentas don't just suddenly stop growing throughout your pregnancy and it would have likely shown small at the 23 week scan.

If you have risk factors for problems with the placenta, getting the placenta assessed by looking at the blood flow and size and shape, may help identify problems early.

As a tree supports life with its branches, the placenta supports the fetus with its nutrients.

Helping loved ones to get through baby loss

If you find yourself in the position where a family member or a friend have lost a baby, or even someone you barely know but want to support, then this chapter is for you.

Firstly, please don't be afraid to say something, hearing "I just didn't know what to say" is the most frustrating and upsetting thing to hear, as recently bereaved parents it is the thing that we heard the most, and it really is so infuriating. It takes two seconds to send a card, or even just a text to say, "thinking of you." If you really can't think of anything to say to bereaved parents, then please just take five minutes to google it.

There is no 'bright side', please do not say <u>any</u> positive platitudes to bereaved parents. There is absolutely no positives or reasons for a child to die. In principle you may think it is a kind gesture, in reality it is *never* welcome I assure you. Positive platitudes do not help bereaved parents at all as they are in such a dark and raw place, the last thing they want to hear is positivity when their whole world has just come crushing down around them.

One of the worst words you could use to a bereaved parent is the word "at least". "At least you can have more children", "at least they are in a better place" or anything that diminishes that person's pain. I assure you that there is no better place for a child to be than with its parents, and children absolutely do not replace other children.

Instead of being positive tell them how awful it is that they are having to go through this horrific pain, tell them that the world is a f*cking cruel place and no one should have to suffer the loss of a child, tell them it's cruel, tell them that you are so sorry for them having to go through this. Make them feel like their pain is seen and validated.

If you are lucky enough to never have had to lay your child to rest then please, absolutely do not tell them how to think, and how you think they should be grieving or thinking. Let them be angry, let them cry, let them shout. I'm sure if your child died you would be doing all of those things too and feeling so much rage and anger. Let them feel it, as how else do you think they should feel? They aren't going to be trying to think positively, they aren't going to be thankful that their child has died.

Everything doesn't happen for a reason so please do not pretend that it does. There is absolutely no reason that babies or children of any age should die. There absolutely isn't. I have heard this saying so many times,

☆

and it is the most unhelpful thing a person can say. It just makes me feel so angry and hurt, and that my pain is unseen and unvalidated. Please remember that the words you use and the things that you say to us will never heal us, so please remember that before you tell us to look on the bright side and that our children are in a better place now.

One thing that you absolutely must remember is that children **do not** replace other children. It is one of the most hurtful things you could say to a grieving parent. I have had so many stupid and hurtful comments said to me, one time I was told that "you are young, and at least you can have more children" you can only imagine how upset I was and how angry that made me. Especially when he followed on to say "I have friends that have been told they can't have children, I think their pain is worse than yours" I shouted at him and cried. It played in my head over and over again. How an earth can you say that you think one persons pain is worse than someone else's? Why would you even say that. To the griever what they are going through is the absolute worst thing imaginable, and you're telling them that their pain is not big enough? Please do not compare one person's pain and grief to another. There is no right time to have that conversation with a grieving parent.

If you are worried to bring up their child because it will upset them, please do not. In most cases bereaved parents love nothing more than talking about their children. They are still their parents after all. You will

☆

not make them sad by "reminding" them their baby died. I assure you it is not anything you can be reminded of because it's something we will never, ever forget. And we wouldn't want to, our babies are still our whole entire world whether they are living or not.

What you can do, of course, if they are ready, is talk to them about their baby, ask them questions about their births, ask to see photos of them. Include them in celebrations, include them in cards, buy the families keepsakes with the name of their child on. There is nothing more I love than receiving gifts and cards with Eli's name on. It makes me feel that he is loved, thought of and most importantly remembered.

We had Eli's name put on a plaque in the children's part of a cemetery and Eli has taken over a part of that garden now with all his little ornaments, wind chimes and other bits and pieces. We call it Eli's Garden and it is such a special place for us to go to. Eli's Nanny and Aunty visit there weekly to tidy it, and make it look lovely. On different holidays and special occasions, they and other family members leave cards and gifts, and it is honestly the most beautiful thing to see and it leaves Dean's and my hearts feeling so full.

It really warms my heart to know that Eli is still thought of by everyone and it just proves how loved he still is. There is nothing more special than knowing that your child is still loved and remembered by so many people. Whether it's been one month, or fifteen years I can assure you if their children's names are spoken of, it will make their absolute day. Just knowing that they have not been forgotten means the absolute world to us.

If someone you know is going through child loss, or grief of any kind just please remember that your words do not heal them nor or they supposed to. Just be there for them, listen to them, and support their choices, and above all make their pain feel validated and that their pain is seen.

Be present and empathetic: Offer a listening ear and be available to support your loved one. Let them express their emotions and validate their feelings without judgment. Avoid trying to fix or minimize their pain, but instead, be a compassionate presence.

Use sensitive language: Be mindful of the words you use when discussing their loss. Use their baby's name if given and avoid euphemisms or dismissive phrases. Respect and acknowledge the significance of their loss.

Offer practical assistance: Grief can be overwhelming, and your loved one might appreciate practical help with day-to-day tasks. Offer to cook meals, run errands, or help with household chores. Small gestures can make a big difference during a difficult time.

Respect their grieving process: Understand that grieving is a deeply personal journey, and everyone copes differently. Respect their need for space and privacy when necessary. Let them know that you are there for support whenever they are ready.

Validate their experience: Acknowledge the significance of their loss and the pain they are going through. Let them know that their feelings are valid and that you are there to support them without judgement.

Remember important dates: Be mindful of important dates like their baby's due date, the anniversary of their loss, or other significant milestones. Reach out to your loved one on these days to let them know you are thinking of them and their baby. It can make such an impact on someone suffering with grief to know that they are seen, their pain is valid and most importantly, their baby is remembered.

Provide resources: Offer information about support groups, counselling services, or resources specifically tailored to individuals experiencing baby loss. They may find solace in connecting with others who have had similar experiences.

Be patient and understanding: Grief doesn't have a timeline, and healing takes time. Be patient with your loved one and understand that their emotions may fluctuate. Offer ongoing support and let them know that you are there for the long haul. And please only offer this if you really mean it. Grief does not end at the funeral or after their first birthday. Grief is ongoing and reoccurs all of the time for the rest of the parent and families' lives. Please remember this.

☆

Remember, everyone's experience of baby loss is unique, so it is important to be sensitive, patient, and attentive to their individual needs. Offering genuine support and being a compassionate presence can make a significant difference during such a challenging time.

Things not to say:

- Time heals all wounds.

- Let go, move on, get over it.

- Have faith.

- Everything happens for a reason.

- Anything that starts with the words "At least".

- God needed another angel.

- They are no longer suffering.

- They are in a better place now.

- Because of you I hug my kids harder.

- You seem happier now.

- What doesn't kill you make you stronger.

- This will make you so strong.

- It just wasn't meant to be.

- God has a plan.

☆

- Any positive platitudes whatsoever. There is nothing positive about a baby dying.

Things to say:

- I am so sorry.

- You don't deserve this.

- Life is cruel.

- Your feelings are validated.

- You have a right to feel how you are feeling

- I would love to hear about your baby when you are ready.

- I would love to see a photo of your baby.

- Your baby is so beautiful.

- Grief has no expiration date.

- You don't have to talk. I will just sit right beside you.

- Talk about your son/daughter whenever you feel like.

- I was thinking of your baby today.

- I saw something and it reminded me of your baby.

- I will never forget your child.

- He/she is so special to me.

- He/she would be so proud of you.

☆

- You are such a good mum/dad.

- Give them permission to be mad as hell.

- You will never 'get over it'.

- There is no right or wrong way to grieve.

-Say their baby's name!!

<u>How to bring up your friend's child in conversation:</u>

- I saw this, and it made me think of *name*

- Have you had any signs from *name* recently?

- Have you done anything for *name* recently?

- I went to visit *name* resting place/ memorial place at the weekend.

- I'm really missing *name*

- I wish *name* could be here to experience this with you.

- I wonder what *name* would be like now and what milestones they would have achieved.

- Will you be celebrating their birthday this year?

- How do you remember them on special occasions/holidays.

- Have something in your home to remember their children by, tell them about them and send photos.

- Light candles for them and send them a photo, to let them know their children are being thought of.

- Keep a note of special dates of their children, birthdays etc. Send a card to know they are remembered.

- Send a photo of any signs you have received from their children, or anything that makes you think of or remember them. Perhaps they have a special symbol such as a butterfly, animal or flower for their child, take photos when you see one, or buy them a gift with their special symbol on it.

- Reach out to them when their child should be starting a new chapter in their lives such as first day of school, let them know they are being thought of.

- Any time you see their child's name let them know, take a photo of it and send it to them.

- Do something special for their child such as plant some flowers to symbolise them or done to a charity in memory of them.

I absolutely love it when someone messages me about Eli, if they have seen something that symbolises him for example or a sign from him. I screenshot each one and print them off and put them in his scrapbook. Knowing he is still remembered and loved and cared for means the absolute world to me and his daddy.

If you hesitate to mention a child who has passed away, fearing it will cause sadness by bringing up their death, remember this:

They haven't forgotten their child.

What you're truly doing is honouring their memory by acknowledging that they lived, and that is a precious gift.

Getting through the holidays

Each holiday and milestone that comes up, sometimes can feel like the grief process has started from the beginning again. It can be such a hard and overwhelming time, just getting through the days can sometimes feel impossible. But please remember that although your child is not here physically, and you can't see or hear them, they are still with you spiritually. They are with you in everything you do, and they will always be a part of your family no matter what.

Each holiday period can be such a hard time for us bereaved parents. It's another experience our children have missed out on, and sometimes the pain is just too unbearable. There are so many things that can trigger us on daily basis in the lead up to all holidays. What would my baby be doing if he was here? What would he dress up as at Halloween? Where would we have taken him to watch the fireworks? What would we have brought him for Christmas? There are so many questions and so many what ifs.

☆

There is no right or wrong way to do life as a grieving parent. If you want to cancel your Christmas, etc then by all means do what is good for you.

The way I look at it, is that although my baby won't be experiencing Christmas with us like he should be, he also wouldn't want to see his mummy and daddy wallowing in pain and self-pity over a holiday we once found so exciting. He would want to see us being as joyful as we can, and to find ourselves a bit of peace knowing that he is with us and watching over us still.

I will continue to include Eli as much as I can over the holiday periods. This Halloween was the first Halloween I have experienced without him, as I was pregnant still with him last Halloween. I carved pumpkins for him, I made a Halloween craft with his footprints I have had put on a stamp, I brought him a Halloween Mickey Mouse dressed up as a pumpkin with his name embroidered on his ear. I painted him a plastic pumpkin and put his name on there too and as a family we all decorated his garden with Halloween bits and pieces.

This Christmas I will also make lots of things with his name on, I will decorate his garden with the family, I will buy him presents and I have also told our family that we still want him included in our Christmas cards, and if they wish to buy him anything we would be more than grateful. I have ordered him a stocking which I will put all of his cards in. I will save him a spot at the dinner table with his photo on and a candle lit for him. I also brought the stamp with his hand and footprints on so I can stamp any birthday and Christmas cards we write, so he is always going to be included.

Trying to find joy at Christmas will no doubt bring a lot of feelings of guilt, and it will be a very challenging time for us all, feeling like we shouldn't be joyful because Eli isn't here with us, where he should be. But the guilt won't make us feel any better, and Christmas is going to happen whether we want to be a part of it or not. The only way I can bring myself joy is remembering Eli and making sure that he is still a part of the family and the celebrations we choose to have.

It's important to do what is best for you and your family on any holidays, if you don't want to take part in big family events and you just want to get away from it all or ignore it, then do that if you feel you need/want to. You need to ensure that you put yourselves first, nothing else matters.

<u>Things to do in the lead up to Christmas:</u>

- Be gentle to yourself and your family.

-Don't give yourself too many expectations.

- Come off social media if it will trigger you, seeing other families and children celebrating at Christmas time.

- Do what you feel called to do when it comes to celebrations.

☆

- Speak to your partner, and family about how you wish the day to go.

- Think about ways to include your children at Christmas, there are so many lovely, personalised decorations you could purchase for them, or sentimental baubles you could collect.

- Think about how you want the day itself to go and if/how you want to include your children.

- Let your friends and family know if you wish that your child is included in Christmas cards and presents beforehand, some may not know what to do so clarifying this is beneficial, so you won't get upset on the day thinking your child has been forgotten.

Ways to remember your baby at Christmas:

- Include their name in holiday traditions: Incorporate your baby's name into your holiday traditions. You can say their name during family prayers, include it in a toast, or share stories and memories about them during gatherings. Keeping their memory alive in your conversations can be a meaningful way to honour them.

- Hang a special ornament: Create or buy a personalised ornament that represents your baby or their name. Hang it on your Christmas tree as a symbol of remembrance and love. You can also include their birthstone or a small photo in the ornament.

☆

- Light a memorial candle: Set up a designated area in your home where you can light a candle in memory of your baby throughout the Christmas season. Take moments of reflection and quiet contemplation as you remember them.

- Create a memorial stocking: Hang a stocking for your baby alongside the other stockings in your home. You can fill it with small tokens, letters, or mementos that represent your love and remembrance for your baby.

- Write a letter to your baby: Take some time during the holiday season to write a heartfelt letter to your baby. Share your thoughts, feelings, and wishes for them. You can place the letter in a special box or read it aloud as a way of connecting with their memory.

- Donate or volunteer in their honour: Consider donating to a baby loss charity or volunteering your time to support others who have experienced a similar loss. This act of giving can be a meaningful way to honour your baby's memory and help others in need.

- Create a memorial display: Set up a special display in your home that includes photos, candles, and other items that remind you of your baby. It can be a dedicated space where you can spend time reflecting on their life and the impact they had on you and your family.

- Reach out for support: Seek support from friends, family, or support groups during the holiday season.

☆

Sharing your feelings, memories, and stories with others who understand can provide comfort and solace.

-Create a memorial decoration: Craft or create a special decoration that represents your baby. It could be an ornament, a wreath, or a display that you incorporate into your holiday décor.

- Volunteer or support others in need: Engage in acts of kindness and support in honour of your baby. Volunteer at a local shelter, donate gifts to children in need, or participate in fundraising events that align with causes that are meaningful to you and your baby.

- Spend time thinking of your child: If you have made your baby a memory box, open the box during the holiday season to reminisce and reflect on your baby's memory.

- Do something in their memory: You could do something such as a sponsored walk. You could do this on your own, with your partner or also with friends and family to remember your little one.

- Find a new hobby in memory of your baby: You could do something such as knitting, you could then create things to donate to baby loss charities such as knitted blankets or teddys.

- Do a special activity in remembrance of your baby: This could include your whole family if you have other children as well, you could create pictures and cards for your angel baby.

Most people want presents under their tree.

My wish is different, every year I wish that you were here with me.

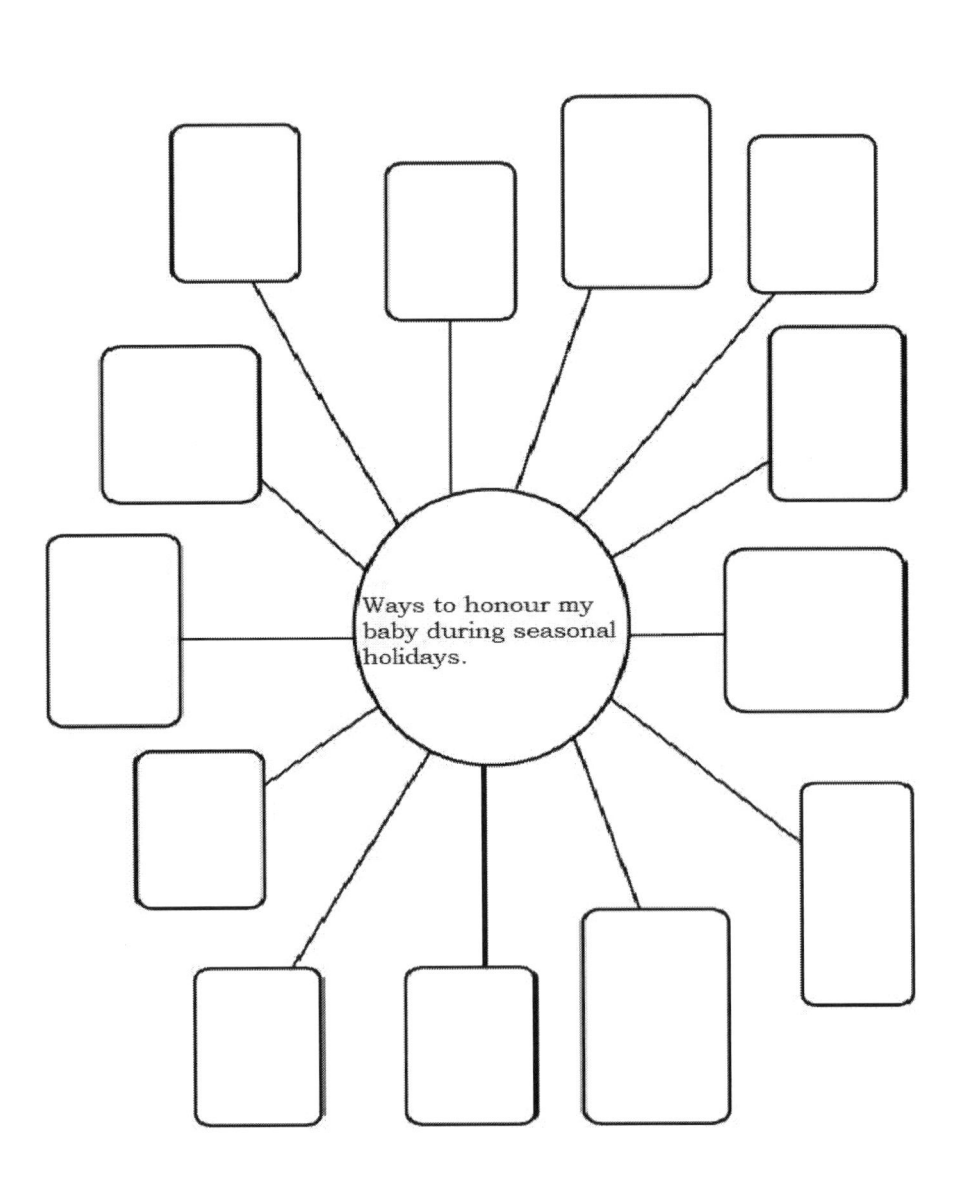

Ways to honour my baby during seasonal holidays.

There's a little place within my heart,
That is with me every day.
A place where all my memories
Are softly tucked away.
It is the perfect place,
In my grief for me to go,
For words could not explain
How very much I miss you so.
And now that once again
Christmastime has come around,
It's where the sweetest memories,
And thoughts of you are found.

Eli's 1st Birthday

Eli's upcoming First birthday is creeping up now that he is eleven months old. It has been such a hard time for me on the lead up to his birthday, and in true Chelsey style the best way I cope is by keeping myself busy.

I am planning a starlight walk for Sands Charity three days before his birthday, at Nonsuch Park where Eli has his bench. It is going to be a family occasion where we can all walk and remember Eli. We have paper lanterns to carry with us, we are going to have sparklers for Eli to enjoy watching, and we are going to release balloons for him also.

I was going to do it on his actual birthday, but then Eli's daddy and I decided against doing it on his actual birthday, as we do not know how either us will be mentally on that day. So, on his actual birthday the 13th December we are going to be having a little tea party at one of his Nanny's houses in the evening with our intimate family members.

I'm going to make him a Lion King birthday cake, decorate his Nanny's house with balloons and banners and try to make it a nice evening as much as we possibly can for him. We are also going to get some fireworks for him to watch from the sky. I am not looking forward to having to do his first birthday without him, however again, I have no choice so the only way I can get through it, is thinking of all these different ideas to do, to get myself through the lead up and the day. We will of course go and visit his garden on his birthday, and his bench also.

I will be getting him birthday presents still, and a card and I will try and make it a day that will be remembered by us and Eli forever. I am also asking our family members to do the same, whether it be an ornament for his memory shelf or garden, or a donation to a baby loss charity. I will keep all the cards he receives in the upcoming years in his memory box.

The way I am choosing to celebrate Eli's birthday may seem unconventional to some, but so is my motherhood. I've decided that again like Christmas, I can either sit and wallow all day and cry about my baby not being here (which no doubt I will also be doing) or I can try and put my pain into purpose and focus on making it the best as I can for my little Eli. In hope that he is there with us, enjoying his birthday celebrations with us.

Eli died two days before he was born, so to me it's his birth date and not the day he died. I like having clarification between those two dates. However, it is different for some babies where they died on the day they were born. If it is your baby's birthday coming up then please do what you feel is best for you and your family. Some people may want to just grieve alone with their loved ones, and that's ok. Do whatever you feel is best for you and your families. There is no right or

☆

wrong way to do this, so please go with what your heart says and most importantly be kind to yourself.

Ideas to honour your baby on their birthdays:

- Hold a memorial gathering: Invite close family and friends to come together and remember your baby on their first birthday. You can share stories, memories, and moments of reflection. Consider incorporating symbolic moments like lighting candles or releasing balloons.

- Visit a special place: Take a trip to a meaningful location associated with your baby. It could be a place you visited during your pregnancy or a location that holds sentimental value. Spend time there, reflecting on your baby's memory and finding solace in the surroundings.

- Write a letter, message or card: Write a heartfelt letter or message to your baby, expressing your love, hopes, and dreams. Share your emotions and thoughts as you commemorate their birthday. You can choose to keep the letter for yourself or read it aloud as a way of connecting with their memory.

- Release lanterns, balloons, or butterflies: Consider releasing lanterns or butterflies as a symbolic gesture on your baby's birthday. Watch them soar into the sky or flutter away, representing the spirit and memory of your baby.

- Create a memory project: Engage in a creative project in memory of your baby. It could be a scrapbook, photo album, artwork, or a personalised keepsake. This project can be a tangible representation of your love and a tribute to their birthday.

- Donate or volunteer: Make a charitable donation or engage in volunteer work in your baby's name. It can be a way to spread love and support to others while honouring your baby's legacy.

- Plant a tree or flower: Consider planting a tree or a special flower in memory of your baby. This act of growth and nurturing can symbolise the life and love that continues to flourish, despite their physical absence.

- Host a fundraising event: Organise a fundraising event or participate in one to support a baby loss charity or a cause that holds significance to you. This can create a lasting impact and provide support to other families who have experienced similar loss.

- Seek support and connection: Reach out to support groups, online communities, or counselling services. Connecting with others who have experienced similar loss can provide understanding, comfort, and a sense of community during this emotional time.

- Talk to your family and friends about how you want to celebrate your child's birthday, if you want to at all. Plan what you would like to do and let your friends and family know. For example, if you wish to receive gifts and cards in memory of your baby, let them know.

The way you choose to remember your baby on their first birthday, or any other birthday should reflect your personal feelings and desires. Take the time you need to grieve, remember, and celebrate their life in a way that brings you healing and comfort.

Ways to honour my baby on their birthday

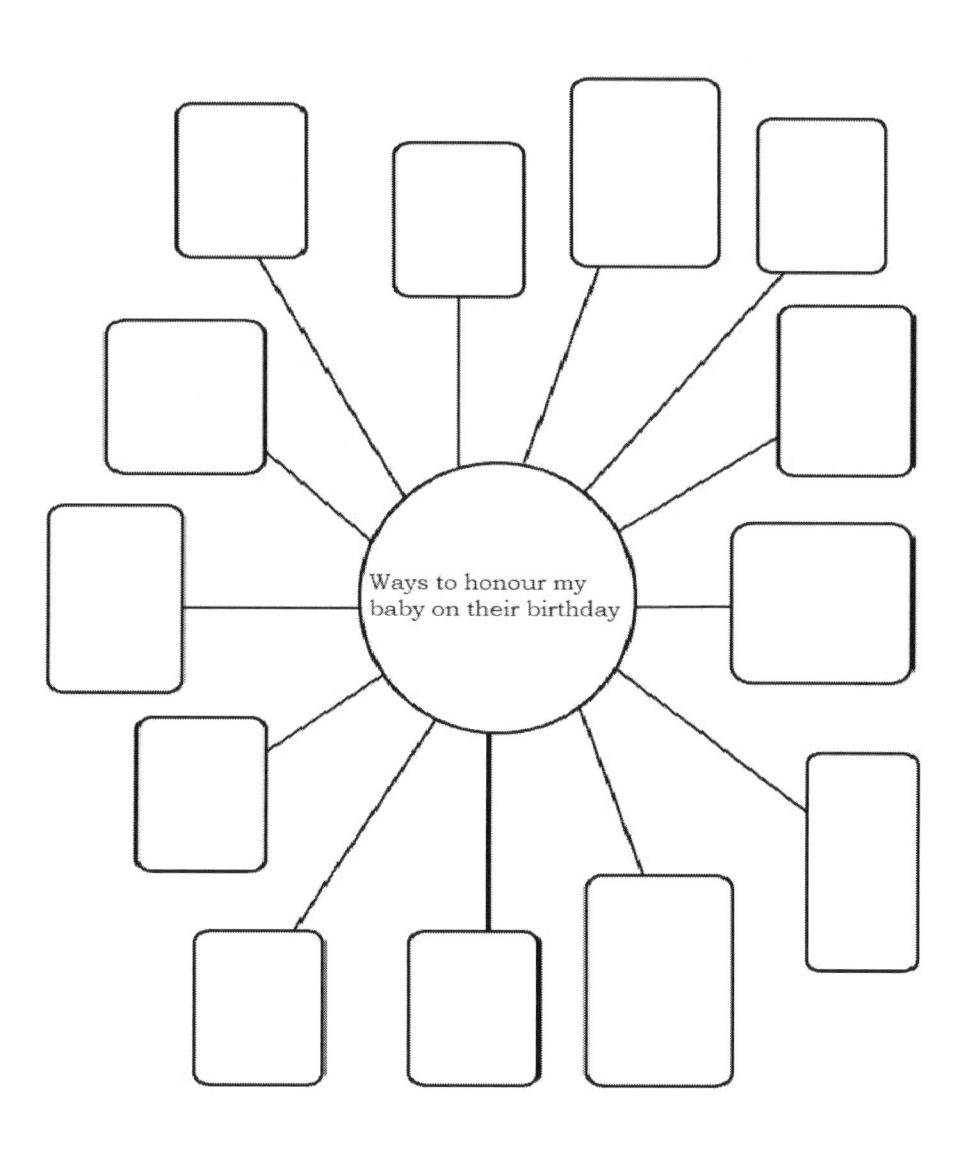

☆

My eyes are filled with tears again,

As I stand here where you lay.

I think of you every second,

But miss you every day.

My body is full of sadness,

That you are no longer here.

Pain is only soothed,

By the memories I hold so dear.

My tired heart is broken.

And doesn't beat the same.

And it breaks a little more,

Every time I hear your name.

My dreams are of the future,

When I no longer feel this pain.

I'll follow you up to Heaven,

And we will meet again.

☆

I love you to the moon & back, to infinity & beyond

Happy 1st Birthday my beautiful Eli, we hope you have the best day with all your friends in the stars. We love you to the moon and back again, to infinity and beyond.

Signs from Eli

I am not sure about what happens after we die, and if there really is an afterlife. Eli dying broke what should have been the circle of life. And I will never understand how or why he could die before he was even born.

What was the reason for his death? Why do baby's die? None of it makes sense. Since his death I have been researching all different theories about what happens after we die, I've watched videos from mediums explaining what happens and certain things like soul contracts.

Whether or not there is life after death we won't know for sure, until it is our turn to leave this life. However, believing that Eli is still with us in spirit form helps me to heal. Since Eli died we have received so many signs from him to allow us to believe that he is here with us still. Although there is nothing I want more than to be able to see, hear and feel him this is all we have, and this is the way I must parent him. I must believe he's with us, and I am sure with all my heart that he is.

I believe that he is with our loved ones on the other side, and they are there in an instant when you need them or speak to, or about them. That's what I imagine, Eli is flying around with our loved ones and giving us all the signs as and when he can and feels called to. It helps me

☆

to heal, knowing he is with us still and I know in my heart its true.

Why else would an unborn baby die in an instant? Surely there is a reason for it and another life out there somewhere. I am going to use this chapter in the book to speak about the moments I have had with Eli. How I choose to parent him after death, and how it has helped me to heal.

When Eli first died we were a mess. Everything just felt so wrong. When I smiled or laughed for a second I just felt pure guilt. Guilt that he should be here, and not me. It took a while for me to be able to appreciate the connection we still had, and the mother and son relationship we would get to have with each other, even though he is not here with us physically.

We were connected from the moment he started growing in my tummy, his DNA still runs through my body to this day. So why would we not be together still. How is it possible to not be together still when our souls have been intertwined together for such a long time.

Once I started appreciating having Eli in my life, and stopped punishing and blaming myself he really came through, and some of the signs we've had from him have just been phenomenal. The day I accepted what had happened, and that it was out of my control, and I stopped blaming myself so much, and promised Eli I would enjoy life for him, that's when things really started happening and I started noticing things.

☆

In the early days of my grief, the days that I was the rawest, the days I would scream in a pillow and cry or sit on Eli's bedroom floor and wail. The days I felt like I couldn't go on. I would ask Eli to give me strength, to get me through another day.

I didn't notice at the time, but once I asked him to give me strength, I had a bout of energy from nowhere. I picked myself up from the floor, and the strength came to me from nowhere. Each time I asked Eli to give me strength to keep going, he did. And I really am grateful to him for that.

I currently live in a flat which is on the third floor. When I was pregnant with Eli and I sat at my kitchen table when I was working from home, I noticed that a crow was watching me all the time from the tree outside my window. So many times, I would see the crow staring at me when I looked up from my laptop screen. It used to make me feel a bit uneasy at first, but it was almost like a comfort like the crow was watching out for me.

When Eli died I noticed that the crow was still watching me from my window every day. Sometimes it wouldn't be there, but it would always appear at times when I was particularly struggling. It was only when I started looking into the meaning of seeing crows that I understood why it kept appearing. People often think crows are a bad omen, but it turns out that they are good omens.

☆

They are commonly believed to represent positive meanings such as transformation, fearlessness, mystery, adaptability, and a higher perspective. Crows show up to let you know that there are spiritual shifts happening around you and remind you to pay attention to the spiritual messages that are sent to guide you.

All birds are spiritually sensitive to energies around the environment, but when I researched the meanings of seeing crows I found out that crows are even more connected to the spirit realm than most birds and are viewed as spiritual messengers.

Other birds I saw a lot whilst pregnant were magpies. We used to count them to work out if we were having a girl or boy, and for some reason every time Dean and I were out together we used to point the magpies out and count them together. I don't know what made us do this, as before I didn't really pay them much attention.

I would say I was very tunnel-visioned before having Eli. Every time I see a magpie when I'm out now, I always say "hello Eli" as I'm sure its him and his way of telling us he's with us. Everywhere we go we seem to see them, one time in the early stages of our grief we went for a walk for the first time down to the beach. It's one of our favourite walks, and every time we turned the corner there was a magpie sitting there, we'd walk past him and then it would be standing there at the next corner as if it was waiting for us.

☆

It was so strange for us, but we are sure it was Eli coming with us on our walk. That was when we had our first conversation about spirituality and the afterlife. There have been so many occasions where I see a magpie and I know it is him, one day I was having so much anxiety as I was walking to the doctors, and a magpie appeared. The magpie was watching me, so I said hello Eli, as I normally do and to my shock it chirped back at me! It turns out magpies are just as spiritual as crows, as they are cousins.

When we were back from the hospital after we had to leave Eli there, Dean and I started standing at Eli's bedroom window to say good night. At first it felt abnormal and wrong to me, I felt strange saying goodnight to someone who is no longer alive. I felt stupid almost as I wasn't sure if he could hear us. But now, it's like a second nature to us. We say goodnight to him every single night from his bedroom without even thinking about it or questioning why we are doing it.

It's almost normal and it is now a part of our daily routine. It's like we know he is listening to us when we speak to him. We talk to Eli about our days and what is going on with us and the family. It's like our own little therapy we do together, taking time out of each day to talk to our son.

When we first started saying good night to Eli we started asking him for signs. Signs that he was ok and being looked after by our past family members and friends.

☆

Firstly, I asked Eli to show us signs of a dolphin, my favourite sea animal and it was just a random thing I thought of.

I watched some medium videos online, and they said that if you want to receive a sign from your loved one, to choose something at random so you know it is a sign from them. I then asked my Grandad Jim also known as James to show us signs of frogs to let us know he was with Eli. That was just another random sign I could think of. Finally, we asked our Nanny Rose (Dean's nan who died around five years ago) before we moved into our flat to ask for signs of a Rose.

The next day I received a few signs and at first I wasn't sure if they were just coincidences, until I got a few and really started to believe. The first sign we saw was a TV advert featuring dolphins, then twice we saw a programme with frogs and finally a friend changed their Facebook profile picture to a rose.

I had entered a crystal giveaway on Instagram a few weeks before and although I hadn't won anything, I got a message from the company apologising that I hadn't won, but they would like to send me something as they saw my story and wanted to gift me something to help put a smile on my face. They sent me a rose quartz crystal and some rose calming spray. A week or so later I got a letter from my husband's cousins wife saying:

☆

"Hi Chelsey,

I went to a new shop near me to look for something for my crystal course and I was drawn to the Rose Quartz. You popped into my head, and I felt drawn to the pendant. I just had to get it for you. About 5 days later, I attended/observed another course. This course was held below a crystal shop in Covent Garden. I found myself looking and smelling aura sprays and room sprays – Again I thought of you, so I purchased the rose mist.

I truly believe in things not being a coincidence and I have this feeling that I was drawn to the "ROSE" and really think Nanny Rose is saying she is with Eli. She is looking after your beautiful boy.

Only today did I realise the significance of posting your gift when I wrote the date 2/2/22 as seeing this number is an angel number. It's an indication of being protected by guardian angels. Also, you might have made the connection that the day we celebrate Eli' is 22/2/22 has this angel number too. Eli is so loved and is so special. The family are looking after him."

All the signs I asked our family for were given, in many ways and I just know in my heart of hearts that they really were listening to us.

Another thing that happened a few days after, when Dean was sorting out his belongings under the bed. He found Nanny Rose's hospital wristband with her NHS number on which we found so strange, as we moved into our flat a while after she died. We think it was the one she was wearing when she died in hospital, but we can't be sure as we have no idea why he would have that wristband and why it would be alone in the middle of the floor under our bed.

The day after Dean and I got married we saw the most amazing thing out of the window. It was Dean that told me to look out the window at the sky and I just couldn't believe my eyes. The clouds had formed what I can only describe as a baby in the sky, it looked exactly like one of Eli's baby scans when I compared them after. And the rays of sun were around the baby clouds as if the sun was shining from him. It was honestly amazing. I'm not sure what made me film the clouds, but I did and when I looked back on the video I can only describe what looked like a dolphin jumping over the baby's face. It was the most amazing thing I've ever seen and honestly, I just couldn't believe my eyes.

Another sign we've had is little white feathers we have been receiving. A medium also confirmed with me in a reading that they were indeed coming from Eli. We've had white feathers appear out of nowhere, one time whilst me, Dean and our parents were at Eli's Garden one dropped from the sky and floated around all our heads, when we looked up there was nothing in the sky and it was as if it literally came from nowhere.

We have had feathers appear from nowhere so randomly, one has come flying out of our kitchen cupboard, in our

⭐

cars, one landed on my shoulder when I was sitting on the bed in our room, Dean's mum had one appear on her kitchen dining table, as well as Dean's aunty on her dining table too.

I also noticed after Eli died, there were orbs in most of the videos taken of me, and some taken by me. There was a video of me in Ibiza on a slingshot and the orb follows me into the sky and back again, there was an orb next to me and Dean on a video from our wedding, and so many more too.

As mentioned before in my letter from Deans cousin's wife, I see angel numbers all the time. An angel number is a repetitive or predictable sequence or pattern of numbers such as 1111, 2222. They are usually 3 or 4 numbers long. But I see them all the time, phone numbers, the time, number plates. When I started to notice them, I realised that they had meanings, and I didn't know a lot about them until the letter I received from her.

The angel numbers I see the most are the numbers 2222. It suggests balance, trust, and alignment. And it is letting me know that someone – either in the physical realm or spiritual domain – is helping me get where I need to go. I know its Eli letting me know he is guiding me and letting me know he is helping me and supporting me.

Dean and I have had a couple of what I can only describe as dream visitations from Eli. One time I dreamt that he was sitting in his bouncer, and I was feeding him with a spoon. He started blowing raspberries at me in my dream, I remember he blew one so strong that it went all in my face. The strangest thing happened, I flinched in my dream as if it had really happened, my face felt wet, and I remember waking up wiping the wetness off my face and my eyes.

I have never experienced anything like it, I could have sworn on my life that I woke up with my face wet from Eli blowing raspberries at me!

Another time I had a dream that I was doing Eli's scrapbook, it was the same day I had a conversation with Dean where we were wondering what Eli would look like when he was older and what colour his eyes would be. When I was sticking his photos in his scrapbook in my dream there were the photos we took of him in the hospital, but there were photos of him growing up and I remember what he looked like in a photo of him as a teenager. The night before my dream Dean also had a dream of Eli where his sister took him out for dinner and took a photo of him and sent it to Dean. The strange thing is that we both described Eli as looking the same in both of our dreams as a teenager.

We have also had other family members tell us about dreams they have had of Eli. Our cousin said that in her dream Eli's shadow was following her, and she was buying a tiger's eye crystal pendant. It was just after Dean and I had a conversation about the colour eyes Eli would have had. Whether he would have had my eyes or

☆

Deans. As a child I described my eyes as "tigers eyes" as I have hazel eyes with orange around the pupil. She also said the night of her dream the main character in the book she was reading was named Dean. The page she had finished reading that night they was describing his eyes. I wondered if it was Eli's way of letting us know he had tigers eye like his mummy and that's why our cousin was looking at the tiger's eye crystals and pendants in her dream.

Me and Dean and other family members have seen his name randomly in books, and car numberplates, even a bus number said "Eli" which someone sent to me which was bizarre as they normally just have numbers on them, it was on his birthday as well. I have had times where the ring I have with Eli's name and birth stone on has gone missing and found somewhere random in our home.

There have been times where his funeral songs randomly started playing, also in places we would never imagine them being played. When we were thinking about getting another beagle I had a random video pop up on my phone about a beagle called Eli. There have been so many instances where our Alexa, or car radio's start playing up and playing random songs which, we know are from Eli, such as the 'Circle of life'. It seems Eli always shows up for his mama when she needs it most! I will forever be grateful for him for showing up!

Our four-year-old nephew talks about Eli all of the time, he was only three when he died and never physically met

☆

Eli, so we are still so surprised how much he speaks of him and how he remembers him so well. He is always drawing pictures of him and writing his name. When he saw a magpie before, Dean's mum pointed at it and said, "Look Charlie it's a magpie" and he started waving at it saying "Eli, Eli!" this was before Dean and I told anyone that we represent Eli with magpies.

One day Charlie was watching random videos on kids YouTube of a man living in Cambodia building a swimming pool and hut. We weren't sure why he had randomly started watching them as he usually just watches kid's programmes. When Deans mum asked why he was watching them, he told her that "Eli sent them down to me to watch" we couldn't believe it when he said this and was shocked.

There are so many other signs I have received from Eli, and I could talk about them forever, but whatever you believe in, take notice of your surroundings, and start looking for signs from your loved ones. I'm almost certain you will receive them. Call out to them when you are on your own, let them know you want to receive signs from them. Give them a chance to provide you with signs and let them verify their existence.

☆

Signs you may receive from your deceased loved ones:

- Being able to feel their presence around you. As if you just know they are with you, and you have the feeling that they are there. It could be a change in the energy around you, feeling something touching your skin, a soft breeze go by, or a sudden change in temperature.

- Losing or misplacing things. When you can't find something you are sure you left in a certain place and they turn up somewhere that seems completely random, it could be your loved one playing tricks on you.

- Strange happenings around the home for example, photo frames off the wall, electrical issues with things such as lights, radios, and phones. Our house phone often rings, and nobody is on the other end of the phone.

- When you can smell their scent, or a scent that reminds you of them.

- Seeing animals and insects such as robins, butterflies and dragonflies.

- Finding special treasures sent from your loved one such as white feathers, coins, and seashells. Also treasures that are significant to your loved one. For example, I have found a letter E randomly on the floor, and I have seen a lion king children's comforter sitting on a wall waiting to be reclaimed.

- Hearing songs that remind you of them.

- Dream visitations. If the dream feels 'real' and you can remember it vividly it is almost definitely a dream visitation. When I had a visitation from Eli I could remember it clear as day, even now. I never usually remember anything I dream about.

- Angel numbers keep appearing to you, they are usually repeating numbers but if you keep seeing the same numbers over again make sure you research the meaning of the numbers you are seeing.

- Seeing orbs or flashes of light in photos, videos, etc.

- Your pets' reactions in certain situations. For example, my dog often stares and barks at what we see to be nothing at times and acts out of character.

- Finding your family members belongings in unusual places.

- Receiving a sign from your loved one that you have specifically asked for.

Never stop keeping an open mind and allow yourself to believe that the signs you are seeing and feeling are from your loved ones. It is one thing that gets me through my grieving process, believing and knowing that Eli is still around me all the time and sending us signs that he is.

Encourage your loved ones to send you signs, ask for something in particular and give them time to be able to communicate it to you. Don't give up searching and waiting as sometimes it may take longer than you expect. Keep asking and they will show up.

Our loved ones are always with us, people die but love doesn't.

SIGNS I'VE RECEIVED FROM MY LOVED ONES.

A place for you to jot down any signs you receive from your loved ones. You'll be surprised when you look back on how many you have received from them.

☆

As I sit in heaven,

And watch you everyday,

I try to let you know with signs,

That I never went away.

I hear you when you're laughing,

And watch you as you sleep,

I even place my arms around you,

To calm you as you weep.

I see you wish the days away,

Begging to have me home,

So I try to send you signs,

So you know you are not alone.

Don't feel guilty that you have life.

Life that was denied to me.

Heaven is truly beautiful,

Just you wait and see.

So live your life, laugh again,

Enjoy yourself, be free.

Then I know with every breath you take,

You'll be taking one for me.

Trying to Conceive After Loss

Deciding when and if to try for another baby is a very hard decision, one that a lot of mums really do feel guilty about. It is completely your choice if you do decide to, but I know it is a question that is spoken about a lot throughout this community. It took me a while to decide to start trying for another baby, I was wrapped up in so much guilt for Eli as I didn't want him or anyone else to feel like I would be replacing him.

It took me a long while to come to terms that we would just be adding to our family, and Eli would be the best big brother and look after his little sibling. If he was alive we weren't planning on him being an only child as I was always certain that I wanted a lot of children. We decided to try again once we had our wedding six months after Eli died.

Trying to conceive after loss has been the second most stressful experiences of my life after losing Eli. It has been the most guilt-ridden experience, worrying in case Eli would think that we are replacing him. Six months of TTC is not a long time compared to others, but after loss it is the most gruelling thing.

☆

After Eli died I was sure I was just not meant to be a mum, that I didn't deserve to be. Many of those self-doubts kept creeping in every time we would get yet another negative test result, or when I would come on my period. I didn't notice until trying for another baby how similar PMS symptoms and pregnancy symptoms are. It is so cruel as you think you are finally there, and bam the next time you have blood in your knickers. Each month when I came on I would cry and sob and tell myself it's because I wasn't good enough. I'm not cut out to be a mum. Of course that's silly, I am a mum, and I will always be a mum to my Eli. The thoughts eat you up though and I just couldn't seem to let go of them.

Sarah has been my biggest supporter throughout this journey after her baby Theodore died just a few days before mine. We were both TTC at the same time, and we were rooting for each other each month that one of us would finally get pregnant. It became torture for the pair of us, the weeks of getting our hopes up and then, here we go she's back again!

I wish now that I didn't tell other people we were trying for another baby. Eli was conceived so quickly; he really was our little miracle baby! I really didn't think it would take as long as it has the second time round. So many people give differing advice which they think will help. The comment "don't stress" was my worst one, as my whole life is one big stress, so how can I not be stressed. If it was easy enough to flip the switch off and stop

☆

stressing about everything, do you not think we would have all done that a long time ago?

After Eli died, I know I let go of myself. I stopped looking after myself as I should have. I stopped drinking water and just giving myself healthy foods to eat. I just couldn't be bothered I didn't feel worthy enough to look after myself when my baby died. Why should I get to be healthy when my baby isn't? That probably hasn't helped with TTC this time round.

When I got pregnant with Eli I was always eating the correct foods, exercising, and just generally taking better care of my health. When your baby dies you lose sense of life and health in general as being important. I was at the stage where I convinced myself that if I died I would be with my son, so why should I bother looking after myself? It took me a long time for my mindset to change. Instead, I started thinking, Eli didn't get a chance to be here and so many other people are fighting every day to be here on this Earth, I won't waste my life whilst I still have it as that is not what Eli would want.

Whilst TTC I was sure I had a miscarriage without even realising I was pregnant. I will never know for sure, however I was on holiday, and I was a week late on my period. I had many symptoms I had when I was pregnant with Eli. I got my hopes up so much I thought it was finally to be, I then got lower back pain and started bleeding, I hadn't experienced back pain like it since I was in labour with Eli. Maybe it was just my period

☆

being really angry at me because I was a week late, and maybe I was just overthinking the whole thing, as I seem to do quite a lot especially since Eli died.

Whether I was pregnant or not, every time I use the toilet at the ice hockey rink we go to I still get triggered and think of that time when I saw the blood in my knickers, and the feelings that came with it. Maybe it was a blessing for me not to know, however if Eli has a brother or sister with him spirit side, that brings me a little bit of comfort to know that he is not alone.

The TTC journey has been horrendous, I am trying to remain hopeful in this journey of my life. I purchased some ovulation sticks which tell you when you are ovulating, and one month later I got those two lines I had been waiting for, in what seemed liked forever.

I am currently in the very early days on this new confirmed pregnancy, and I am scared and anxious trying to hold on to that little bit of hope. Knowing that one quarter of pregnancies end with a baby dying before 12 weeks is really stopping me from holding on to any hope right now. However, I am trying my best not to get too stressed out about it, not get too anxious, and hope this baby has a fighting chance. I know Eli is watching over his baby brother or sister and is being hopeful for me, Eli's going to make the best big brother regardless of the outcome!

I had told people close to me that Dean and I were trying for another baby. Going back, I wish I kept that to ourselves now as we were often being asked the question if I was pregnant yet. The conversations were sad and infuriating as we were both wanting to be pregnant again so desperately it just didn't seem to be happening quickly enough. It followed many self-doubts on my fertility, and if I were ever able to have a living child. When we were first TTC I was fixated on the 'Flo' app which told you when you were ovulating. Which in hindsight was stupid, as when I fell pregnant with Eli according to the app it was in my infertile period. It was only when I started using the ovulation sticks I realised my correct time for ovulating was different to the apps. At first this caused me more panic as again I thought I just wasn't fertile anymore after a few days of panic and stress, the two lines finally appeared to say I was indeed ovulating after all.

☆

Things that may help with fertility:

- Maintain a healthy weight: Being underweight or overweight can disrupt hormonal balance and affect fertility. Aim for a healthy body weight through a balanced diet and regular exercise.

- Eat a nutritious diet: Focus on consuming a variety of fruits, vegetables, whole grains, lean proteins, and healthy fats. Include foods rich in antioxidants, such as berries, spinach, and nuts, as they can help protect eggs and sperm from damage.

- Stay hydrated: Drink an adequate amount of water each day to support overall health and reproductive function

- Exercise regularly: Engage in moderate exercise regularly, as it can help regulate hormones, improve circulation, and reduce stress levels. However, avoid excessive exercise, as it may have a negative impact on fertility.

- Manage stress: High levels of stress can affect fertility. Find healthy ways to manage stress, such as practicing relaxation techniques, meditation, yoga, or engaging in hobbies and activities you enjoy.

- Limit caffeine and alcohol intake: Excessive caffeine and alcohol consumption have been linked to reduced fertility. It's best to limit or avoid these substances when trying to conceive.

☆

- Quit smoking: Smoking has detrimental effects on fertility for both men and women. If you smoke, consider quitting to improve your chances of conceiving.

- Avoid exposure to toxins: Minimise exposure to environmental toxins, such as pesticides, chemicals, and certain household products, which may negatively impact fertility. Use natural and organic alternatives when possible.

- Understand your menstrual cycle: Familiarise yourself with your menstrual cycle to identify the most fertile days. This knowledge can help you time intercourse more effectively.

- Visit a healthcare professional: If you've been actively trying to conceive without success, consider scheduling an appointment with a fertility specialist. They can evaluate your individual circumstances, perform necessary tests, and provide personalised advice.

If you have been trying to conceive for over a year or if you feel as if something is wrong, please seek help from your GP ASAP. Please don't put it off if you are hoping to become pregnant. There are so many different reasons why people are unable to get pregnant and can be easily addressed such as an infection. Please don't be afraid to ask for help and to confide in others also. Infertility happens to around 9 to 15% of couples*, so please ensure you are not alone in this.

*https://www.britishfertilitysociety.org.uk/fei/what-is-infertility/#:~:text=Infertility%20(often%20called%20subfertility)%20is,couples%20will%20have%20fertility%20problems.

Everybody wants happiness and nobody wants pain. But you can't have a rainbow, without a little rain.

Dear Eli

Thank you for choosing me to be your mummy. Thank you for showing me what it was to truly love another human being. Thank you for being my light that guided me on my dark days. So many people speak of you with sadness, and so often people don't want to talk about you. I am so sorry about this. I love speaking about you, I love including you, and I know although you aren't here physically you are around us all the time. I would give anything to be able to see and hear you, but that is asking for the impossible. I may not be able to see or hear you, but I am positive that you are able to see and hear me. Talking out loud to you makes me feel so close to you, I see you in the birds, the butterflies, the feathers, you are around me everywhere we go, and I am so thankful to you for that. You have changed who I am today. You have made me a better person, a better woman. You have made me a mother. You made me realise how strong I am, even though some days I felt so weak. You have taught me how to love, to be empathetic, and to always be kind to others as you never know what someone else is going through. You've made me believe in myself, and you've made me put myself first for once and not care about other people that have spent so many years bringing me down. You've made me realise what really matters, and you have stopped me from being a people pleaser. I speak my mind now; I fight for you and for your memory too. You have made me strong, and I feel like because of you I can get through anything that life throws at me. You've simply made me a better person and I can't thank you enough for that E. I love being your mummy and I wouldn't change that for the world. If somebody said they could take my pain away, but that would mean you never existed. I would refuse. The pain I hold every day because you are gone will never go away, but I have learned to love the pain as it reminds me that you did exist, you do exist, wherever you are right now, I know you are smiling and watching down on me and the family. Thank you for making me a better person and giving me the strength, I needed from you my little lion. One day when we are reunited again, I hope you tell me how proud you are of me. I will never not include you in our family, because you'll always be a part of our family. Always in our hearts and always remembered. I made a promise to you that I would live my life for you, as I would have wished you to live your life so that is what I am doing. I am trying my best to free myself from regret and my inner demons, all to make you proud and proud that I am your mummy. I will always fight for you Eli and always say your name out loud. I am so grateful to all the people you have introduced me to along this grief journey, other amazing mums that are missing their babies in heaven too. I am so thankful for every single one of them for helping me get through. Thank you for guiding me and always giving me hope and reminding

☆

me that the brightest rainbows always appear after a storm. Forever my best boy. I love you so much Eli.

Love from your mummy. xxxx

That first time I saw your heart beating on the scan. The excitement we held, our future we planned.

The first time I felt you kick, everything felt like it was going so quick.

We got your nursery ready, your wardrobe was full, everything was perfect, everything was checked.

Your gender reveal, your baby shower too, the amount of love for you was so real.

Every appointment, every time was just right. No need to worry, but it turned out you were putting up a fight.

My little lion, so perfect and so brave, oh if only you could have been saved.

I remember the day, its etched on my brain, forever it will remain.

☆

We heard those words no one wants to hear. The anger, the guilt, the sadness, and the fear.

How can a parent continue to live, without their child laying in their crib.

Three days we had with you, we held you, we loved you and cared for you too.

Five little fingers, five little toes, and the most perfect, cute little button nose.

We had to say goodbye and leave you there, with strangers no less, it was so hard to bear.

Not knowing where you were, it was all so wrong. My heart was broken, I did not belong.

Shopping for caskets, urns, and flowers, I felt like a coward.

How could I live when my baby is dead? I didn't want to eat or leave my bed. I wanted to be eaten up and be with you instead.

But I had to go on, even though it felt so wrong.

I had to say your name out loud, to make you proud.

☆

For I was the only one, you have always been my son.

You took my heart, but left me your soul, you gave me back some control.

You taught me to be strong, and I knew all along, you would give me your strength and guide me too,

It would always be you that would get me through.

You showed me you were around, so many signs that I'd found.

I got back on my feet, although I will never feel complete.

I wake every day wishing to be with you for one more day.

But every day is new, and I will always have you.

To protect us and guide us, that I can trust.

So, I will live my life for you, the life I would want you to live too.

☆

I hope I make you proud, until it's my time and I'm also in the clouds,

One day we will be together again, that I will depend.

You and me Eli,

Together until the end.

Eli,

Oh, how I wish I could say something to you, to look into your eyes, to see you looking back at me, to smile at me, to hold your hand, to squeeze you tight and tell you daddy's going to look after you forever. I wanted to watch you grow. I wanted to see you sit for the first time, I wanted to see you stand and stumble for the first time, I wanted to see your first steps, I wanted to teach you to ride a bike, I wanted to sit and watch Barney with you, I wanted to take you to soft play and have daddy running around after you on his knees, I wanted to take you to the park to feed the ducks, I wanted to see your face on Christmas morning, I wanted to take you for your first McDonalds, I wanted to take you swimming, I wanted to have amazing daddy and son naps where we pass out on the sofa from too much candy, I wanted to take you to your first Hockey Game so we could bang on the glass and get you your first puck. I wanted to watch you grow, I wanted to buy you your first skateboard, I wanted to buy you adults Vans and watch you fall off your skateboard, I wanted to take you to the movies and drink Coke and stuff our bellies with popcorn. I wanted to take you on your first rollercoaster. I wanted to introduce you to country music hoping you'd love it. I wanted to drop you off at school and cry my eyes out in the car because I'm going to miss you all day. I wanted you to graduate and stand there and be proud of you. I wanted to have our first beer together. I wanted to see you grow. I wanted to see you find the one just like daddy did, I wanted to see you fall in love. I wanted to see you get married. I wanted to see you buy your first house. I wanted to see you have kids. I wanted to be a grandad. I wanted you to look after daddy when he gets old. I wanted you to be there with me until I was done. I wanted to live on in your head as the best daddy and grandad of all time. I wanted YOU.

People say times a healer, but I can promise you that no amount of time can heal your son being ripped from your life within a blink of an eye. Yes, time goes on, but the feelings never go away, the thoughts never go away, my son never goes away. Every day I wonder what would have been and what would have happened, but all I can do is dream, and hope that I would've made Eli Proud. He is and always will be my son my pride and joy and I will love him until my dying day. He is a part of me and always will be. I know he is smiling down on me every single day and looking after me until we meet again. For now, I just hold him in my heart.

I love you Eli James Arthur Tookey x

Dean Tookey, Eli's daddy.

Our beautiful boy.

This ache in our heart

Will never go away.

It will serve as a reminder,

Of our love for you each day.

We dreamed of you and your life,

And all that it would be.

We waited and longed for you to come,

And join our family.

We never had the chance to play,

To laugh, to talk, to wiggle.

We long to hold you, to touch you,

And listen to you giggle.

I'll always be your Nanny,

He'll aways be your Grandad,

☆

You'll always be our Grandson.

A handsome little lad.

But now you're gone…………. but yet you're here.

We sense you everywhere.

You are our sorrow and our joy.

There's love in every tear.

Just know our love goes deep and strong.

We'll forget you never.

The Grandson we had, but never had.

And yet will be forever.

Thinking of you always Eli, our beautiful boy

Love Nanny & Grandad x

Carol & Harry Moore, Eli's Nanny & Grandad.

☆

In loving memory of a special little angel.

To our beloved Eli,

Our time with you was precious,

But sadly cut too short.

There is not a day that goes by,

Without you in our thoughts.

We know you're out there somewhere,

Up above in the twinkling sky.

We can't forget our tender cuddles,

We love you more as time goes by.

Always in our hearts and thoughts.

Love Nanny Sue & Grandad Kevin.

Sue & Kevin Tookey, Eli's Nanny & Grandad.

☆

Our dreams were shattered, hopes undone.

But your memory shines, like the sun.

We hold you close, within our hearts.

And although we're apart, we're never apart.

Remembering your babies

I wanted to include a chapter in this book dedicated to some of the babies that have blessed me with their existence, and their families that I have met on my own journey.

There are hundreds of babies and loss mum's I have not physically met, but I feel like I have known a lifetime. I feel so lucky and blessed to know such wonderful people and have been so honoured to get to know them and of course their children too.

All your babies are so special and mean the world to me. I will forever be grateful to you all for introducing me to them. I will always think of, love, and remember your babies. Thank you for allowing me this space to include them and for sending me some beautiful words for them.

Vincent Ferrin

For some reason this year has hit me harder than most. Exam results, children flying their coop, all new milestones and then the reality that we lost you. The Tsunami, the never-ending grief that hits me when I least expect it, this year is one of them.

Vincent Li, our boy, my heart, left us in 2008. He fought so hard and beyond the odds that were first given. Secrets were told, football results shared and visits from your big brother were your weekly thing. I massaged your feet and watched you smile, you smacked your lips after each feed, to show me how much you enjoyed my milk.

That day we will never forget, hearing you cry, the only and last time. I felt sick, news I could not comprehend. Why? Why was he dying.

We watched helplessly for 16 hours, doctors and nurses at your aid, but the universe had other things in mind. You fought, we cried and still do.

Vincent Li Ferrin, our boy, my heart.

4th Dec 2007 – 6th Feb 2008

Kirsty Ferrin, Vincent's mummy.

Vinnie by Sonny, Vincent's big brother.

Oscar Milner

My darling boy Oscar, you are missed so much I always wonder what you would have been like, no doubt like your 3 brothers. You are soon to be 3 & I know for sure you would be wrecking my Christmas tree this year & being a mischievous toddler with big beautiful blue eyes & cheeky smile. You are always loved & never forgotten. Our perfect little star, up in heaven is where you are, flying high & twinkling bright, our guiding star, our shining light. Twinkle twinkle little star, our perfect little angel is what you are.

Nichola Milner, Oscar's Mummy.

☆

The elite club you never wanted to join.

25th September 2021 I joined a club,
a club I never wanted to join.
On what should have been a happy day,
at 22:15, Atlas Christopher you were born on to this earth.
I welcomed you with open arms,
knowing that you couldn't stay.
My boy, my Titan, my little warrior son,
This was the day that my pain begun.
You came, you saw, you conquered
as your job here in the world was done.
You made me your mummy
and for that I will always thank you.
I really wish you could have stayed
and I got to see all the ways,
In which you would have lived our life,
The way you would have grown,
Heard you laugh and watched you strive.
Instead I had to say goodbye,
And on that day a part of me died inside.
I will always be your mummy,
and you will always be my boy.
So make me proud my titan son
and hold heaven up nice and tall,
With the mightiest of shoulders for one so small.

Rio Demetriades, Atlas's mummy.

Atlas Christopher

Into the breath of the wind, the wet of the raindrops and
the warmth of the sunshine, we let you go,
To rest peacefully amongst the stars and the rainbows.

Hold my hand,
let us say good-bye,
say good-bye, to meet again soon.
We meet today.
We will meet again tomorrow.
We will meet at the source of every moment.

Rio Demetriades, Atlas' mummy.

Tabitha-Rose

My baby girl
I loved you
Every second
I remember
Every kick
Every hiccup
My stretched out body
My damaged nerves
The pains that still come to my womb
The phantom kicks
All of these I will treasure
The bits of you I get to keep
I aged through birthing you
I expected to
I did not expect that sorrow

☆

Would be the reason
Even the pain
The trauma of birthing you
I will hold tightly
When you felt the closest
To hold the pain in a way
Is to hold you
I carry your soul next to mine
I weep that your strong lungs
Never made themselves heard
I hold your blankets close at night
Your footprints will live forever
In the tiny nursery we crafted for you
I whisper your name everywhere I go
I etch it into my body
Rooting it into the garden by our house
I hold your pictures in my minds eye
I carry them in my pockets
I hold the memory of those few hours in the hospital
The moments you were almost alive
I can almost pretend you were
In those moments I prayed
Perhaps God would make your silent heart beat again
Those moments live in my dreams
In those dreams, the sheer force of my will
made you shake off death
Made you open your eyes to see me
Holding your tiny body
In that room we cherished you
Our daughter that we had waited for
Your daddy danced with you, sweet girl
He sang your song to you

☆

I know you didn't hear it
That too I hold tight in my memory
Until the resurrection when I can tell you
You made us something new
Your dad and I
You ushered me into motherhood
Though I still lose you every day
Every time I make a memory
Without you by my side
May I weep for you the rest of my life
If weeping for you
Makes me your mom
Tabitha-Rose

Five months

I know the path to your grave
Better than the one to your nursery
I've sat by you and your angel friends
More than I've sat in the room we made for you
I lead people to your patch of earth
With a confidence I'm not used to having
There you are
My daughter
And I show them to you
In whatever way I can
I have a hard time not zoning into the world in my head
Here next to you
Words come and if I lose them
Maybe I lose any connection I have to you
So I sit in silence while written words
Are captured here forever

☆

So that you might be
Captured here forever.
Baby girl,
It's so quiet here. If you were awake, I would hold you and point out the peach tree leaves that are starting to turn orange. And we would guess which birds were calling out to each other. It's a little chilly. Oh sweet girl I would snuggle you so hard. I can feel you in my arms if I squeeze them hard enough I don't know if you would babble to me, or if you would calmly take in the silence. You would hold your neck up, and your eyes would look at me. I bet they are blue.
Lillian came with me, today. We cried and ate strawberries and watched the sun set until it got too cold. And talked about who you were. Who you are. It's so peaceful there. Your grave is truly my favorite place to sit and be still. And the drive home through the tree tunnels is perfect and beautiful.
Tomorrow you will be 5 months. And I will be be five months closer to holding you again. Even though sometimes it feels like I am five months further.
I don't leave you when I leave this place. But even so, I'll be back to sit with you again, soon.
Mommy loves you, Tabbi-Rose.

Mallory Martin Stacy, Tabitha-Rose's mummy.

A moment in our arms, a lifetime in our hearts.

Cooper Valentine

So go and run free with the angels

Dance around the golden clouds

For the lord has chosen you to be with him

And we should feel nothing but proud

Although he has taken you from us

And our pain a lifetime will last

Your memory will never escape us

But make us glad for the time we did have

Your face will always be hidden

Deep inside our hearts

Each precious moment you gave us

Shall never, ever depart

So go and run free with the angels

As they sing so tenderly

And please be sure to tell them

To take good care of you for me

Georgia Valentine, Coopers mama.

☆

It must be very difficult
To be a man in grief,
Since "men don't cry" and "men are strong"
No tears can bring relief.

It must be very difficult
To stand up to the test,
And field the calls and visitors
So she can get some rest.

They always ask if she's alright
And what she's going through.
But seldom take his hand and ask,
"My friend, how are you?"

He hears her cry in the night
And thinks his heart will break.
And dries her tears and comforts her,
But "stays strong" for her sake.

☆

It must be very difficult

To start each day anew.

And try to be so very brave-

He lost his baby too.

Dedicated to Jake Valentine, Coopers Dada from Coopers Mama Georgia Valentine.

Jase Hemmings

My darling baby Jase.
You are my son, the angel I was sent. From the day you left my arms, I wondered where on earth you went.
How much I've wailed on your bedroom floor, into the morning, daddy has had to pick me up once more.
My son, how do I keep living knowing how I'll never see you again or feel your touch.
Knowing your feet will never touch the ground. You'll never crawl, walk, talk or even make a sound.
But your mummy, I will always be.
Always wondering and dreaming of who we would have been.
My strong brave little boy, how proud I am of you. How I love you each day that little bit more, until I get to see you.
Sleep tight my darling, you will always be, my sweet baby Jase.

Chloe Bethan, Jase's mummy.

Matilda Lola Adams

Artwork by Marie Hillyard-Adams, Matilda's mummy and Henry, Matilda's big brother.

Artwork by Henry, Matilda's big brother.

Kody Cameron Brown, Tinkerbell and Scarlett

You are one of Heaven's angels now
A perfect little star.
And when you shine the world can see
How beautiful you are.

May you fly with magic wings
On clouds so soft and white.
May your heart be joyful
And your days be bathed in light.

And though our hearts are broken
And your life was far too short.
We thank you, sweetest angel,
For the happiness you brought.

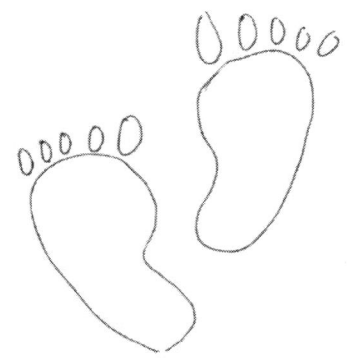

THOUGH WE NEVER HELD YOU
IN OUR ARMS WE WILL
ALWAYS HOLD YOU IN OUR
HEARTS

Brooke Saunders, mummy of Kody, Tinkerbell and Scarlett.

☆

Leo Jon Devlin

Beautiful Orange Sunsets

Our beautiful baby boy Leo,
your arrival took our breath away,
we wished we could have given it to you,
so that you could have stayed.

To make 98 days last a lifetime,
is a pain we cannot comprehend,
grief is a piece of you we get to keep,
so, we've let it become our friend.

The tears they come and go,
the heart ache, it does not follow,
our love for you is so intense,
the same power is in our sorrow.

Without knowing, in that short time,
you gave us your strength to fight,
you coloured strength in orange,
and began to leave us signs.

Your fiery personality lit the sky,
a night we will never forget,
30th January 2022,
you sent us your first orange sunset.

That's not the only gift you've sent us,
from the sky you now call home,
thank you for our beautiful rainbow,

☆

someone we wish you could have known.

Mia, meaning 'mine',
but we know that she is yours,
a rainbow can't exist without a sky,
the sunrise to your sunset, we are sure.

Your second birthday came and went,
missed milestones break our hearts,
we watched your orange sunset over Birmingham Stadium,
reminded, we will never truly be apart.

Until we meet again, our little boy,
we'll introduce you to people you won't meet,
tell them how you left the biggest footprints in our lives,
with such perfect, tiny, little feet.

In our hearts, in our minds, you will grow with us,
your footprints will be made beside ours,
that doesn't mean that we won't miss you,
every single second, every minute and every hour.

Rest peacefully and fiercely, our little lion Leo,
orange will always be our colour of strength,
keep on lighting up the sky and we promise,
to always look for your beautiful, orange sunsets.

Written by Jemima Hughes, for Leo Jon Devlin, from Mummy (Niki), Daddy (Chris) and Sister (Mia).

☆

Theodore Christopher Skelding

Hi Theodore,

God it's hard without you. I miss your face and your smell and the little blemish on your chin and the little hairs that were on your ears. I remember everything about you. The way your skin felt when I touched it. Your hands still felt warm. I'd have held your hand forever if I could have. I wish I could have heard your cry or your little laugh and not just have to imagine what it would have been like. I hope you're looking down on me and know how much I love you and miss you, gorgeous boy. I can't believe it's been 2 years without you. The last thing I said to you in the hospital was that I knew you'd make me stronger, and you've shown me strength I didn't know I was capable of, so thank you for that angel.
I still see you and feel you everywhere, whether that be at your resting place, in the moon and stars or a robin or rainbow. I know you're still here with us watching over us all. Your little sister Sienna was born on the 5th October 2023, and we talk about you all the time to her. Her favourite teddy is our Theodore bear and she's always trying to cuddle you. I know she will be so proud to have you as a big brother when she's older. Thank you for bringing her to us and keep on protecting her please! She's so lucky to have her own little guardian angel looking after her.
You'll always be my first-born baby and I will never hide you away, we will make sure to keep your memory going for as long as we are on this earth. Thank you for

☆

making me a mum T, it's my favourite job. It's a privilege to have felt a love like this. Mummy, Daddy and Sienna love you with all our hearts. I'll always keep searching for you until we are together again. Keep shining angel.

'For nothing loved is ever lost, and he was loved so much.'

Sarah Wrigley, mummy of Theodore.

Lenny Prestwich

Dear Lenny,

Often when people struggle to find words themselves, they borrow them from great thinkers – so here are some from my mum: 'I don't think there has ever been a baby in the whole history of the world who has been loved, cherished and thought about as much as Lenny.' And as you know, my mum is always right.

We started our journey into parenthood as we meant to go on – showing you richness of experiences and unconditional love. Dad enjoyed speaking to you everyday, giving you high fives and playing you music. We knew early on you were a character when you stubbornly refused to change position on scans – we can't fathom how a child of ours could be stubborn! You cycled many miles in mum's tummy, this rocked you to sleep, - like us, you were always happiest on two wheels.

☆

At 6 months mum took you on a cycle tour from Newcastle to Edinburgh – instilling a sense of adventure was always important for us.

Your dad chose your name, he loved it. From 6 months he started calling you Lenny and it stuck. You were never going to be Leonard, just Lenny. Your name needed to be unusual enough so that dad had never taught a child with your name and cool and memorable enough for when you would become a famous mountain biker. As soon as we saw your perfect face we knew it fitted. It means brave as a lion – you certainly have showed us that you are. Roshan was your great grandad's name and means shining light – you will always be a shining light in our lives and brighten our Northern Sky.

You are more beautiful than either of us could ever have imagined – and all that blonde hair really took us by surprise. We didn't know that a baby could look so perfect or that a member of our little family could be better looking than Bella. We will treasure the photos we have of you and the moments we held you in our arms forever.

You have shown us that we have a much greater capacity for love than we ever realised. We thought we would teach you the value of kindness but instead your short life has shown the love and kindness around us. You've taught us so much about ourselves, courage and gratitude, we have no doubt you will continue to shape us as people.

☆

Lenny, there is so much love for you and we have felt that from all around us for the last 9 months. We are so sad you didn't meet the wonderful people we share our lives with. We hope you know how much these special people were anticipating your arrival and the exciting plans they had in store for you.

We are determined to be the best parents we can be. We will take you on adventures in our hearts and live our lives to the full as you weren't able to. Everything we do from now will be in your honour and we hope we can make you proud. We will love each other fiercely and treat others with the level of gentleness and kindness that we have received in recent weeks.

Your memory will be everlasting in our hearts, in the constellation of Sagittarius and on the top of Stanage edge where we will scatter your ashes (in our humble opinion, one of the most beautiful places on earth).

Our pain won't last forever but our love will. Your Mum and Dad.

Mim and Roy Prestwich, Lenny and Bhai's mummy and daddy.

Bhai Prestwich

Little Bhai,
You gave us hope at a time when then world was the darkest place imaginable. Bhai is the name we gave to you, our second son - it means brother in Hindi.

☆

You look just like your older brother Lenny and therefore just like your amazing dad. Your tiny little feet were a perfect replica of Roy's. Your perfectly formed little face looked just like his dad and his brother. Perfect little boys. You brought us so much hope, joy and love and I am devastated you didn't get to stay.

I will never understand why we lost two perfect boys in such random, unrelated and different circumstances, it will never make sense. We hope you are together looking out for each other and going on adventures.

We love you and always will,
Mum and Dad.

Mim and Roy Prestwich, Lenny and Bhai's mummy and daddy.

Viola Testa

Dedicated to our daughter Viola Testa 12.11.21

Twinkle twinkle little Viola
How we wonder what you are,
Up above the world so high
I look for signs of you in the sky,
Twinkle twinkle little Viola
How we wonder what you are.

When the days we lost you were dark
Then we saw your little spark,

☆

Shades of purple, blazing high
Letting us know you were up there in the sky.
Though we now have to live apart
I know I'll always carry you in my heart.

Twinkle twinkle was our special song
When we said goodbye I didn't feel so strong
And living here without you just feels so wrong
How I wish you could have stayed with me
Now you're our angel flying free, we hope you look down on us and you'll see.

Twinkle tinkle little Viola
How loved forever and always you'll be.

Written by Cristina Testa May 2022.
Adapted lyrics and stanza from twinkle twinkle little star author Jane Taylor (17-83-1824)

Violas Mummy, Cristina Testa.

Maila Angela Viana Morais

To Maila Angela,

Though the world may not see you,
you are my constant
from the moment I conceived you,
I made a vow to never let you go and whether I scream it from the rooftops or whisper it in my heart my child you'll remain
The deepest love I can't contain

☆

My first true love
Made within me
And without me you could not be
I'm proud to call you mine
Thank you for your time

And because the world cannot see you,
they often quickly think
How could she miss something she did not live
How could she miss something that never happened
After all, to them without you I'm right back to where
I've always been
In a world where there is no you

But within me you created many worlds
You lived in my sea
You were rooted to me
You were at the core of existence
Where the universe meets, expands and creates
You were living in the most powerful superpower
There's no bigger bang than your conception
You transformed me

So how could they possibly think
I'm right back to the old me?
It may look like I gave birth to you
But really you gave birth to me
And to you I'm forever indebted my sweet child
Forever yours I'll be

Maila's Mummy, Helena Morais.

Orlando and Shiloh Davis

To our beautiful son Orlo,

You are everything we ever hoped for and wanted. A little brother to your older sister. You are a dream to our family. You give us so much love, passion, and joy. The 38 and a half weeks of carrying you inside my tummy and the two weeks of having you alive in this world I will cherish forever.

The day you left to become an angel on the 24th September 2021 was the most excruciating day of our lives. I have peace that you were no longer suffering. You fought a battle amazingly and so bravely every step of the way. You are my hero.

Having to let go of the beautiful person I created and longed for, well the pain is just indescribable. Something that no parent should ever experience. The pain will be carried with us forever. I will, however, fully embrace this pain because that pain is simply the price to pay for love. The heavy grief I carry is just the heavy love we have for one another.

This journey hasn't been easy for our family and every bit of fight we do is to get justice for you. Your passion shines through me and your name is being heard. Orlando you are already saving so many lives from your story, but I am so so sorry it took your life for this to happen.

☆

In March 2023 we entered further despair when your little sister Shiloh joined you up in the sky straight from my tummy.

Motherhood with a baby in the sky is being loved from every angle. It's being guided by your children at all times and your angels being with you in every single moment of life. That to me is such a comfort I hold on to, to know I'm never alone, even in the loneliest of moments.

We wonder about you both every minute of the day. We see you both in our days and our nights. You're the little robin that stops by to send us messages. To the twinkling stars up above, to the beautiful big beautiful blue sky, to the white feathers, to the blue flowers, all the incredible signs that we know you are present with us.

I learnt that mothers carry their babies DNA inside their bodies forever and I find such peace in having you both inside me chemically forever. An unbreakable bond.

Forever and always my beautiful, precious babies. You make me so proud to be your mother and I miss you dearly. We talk about you both constantly, we celebrate your lives, your siblings will always look up to you and I hope we all make you proud.

Love from Mummy.

Orlando and Shiloh Davis' mummy, Robyn Davis.

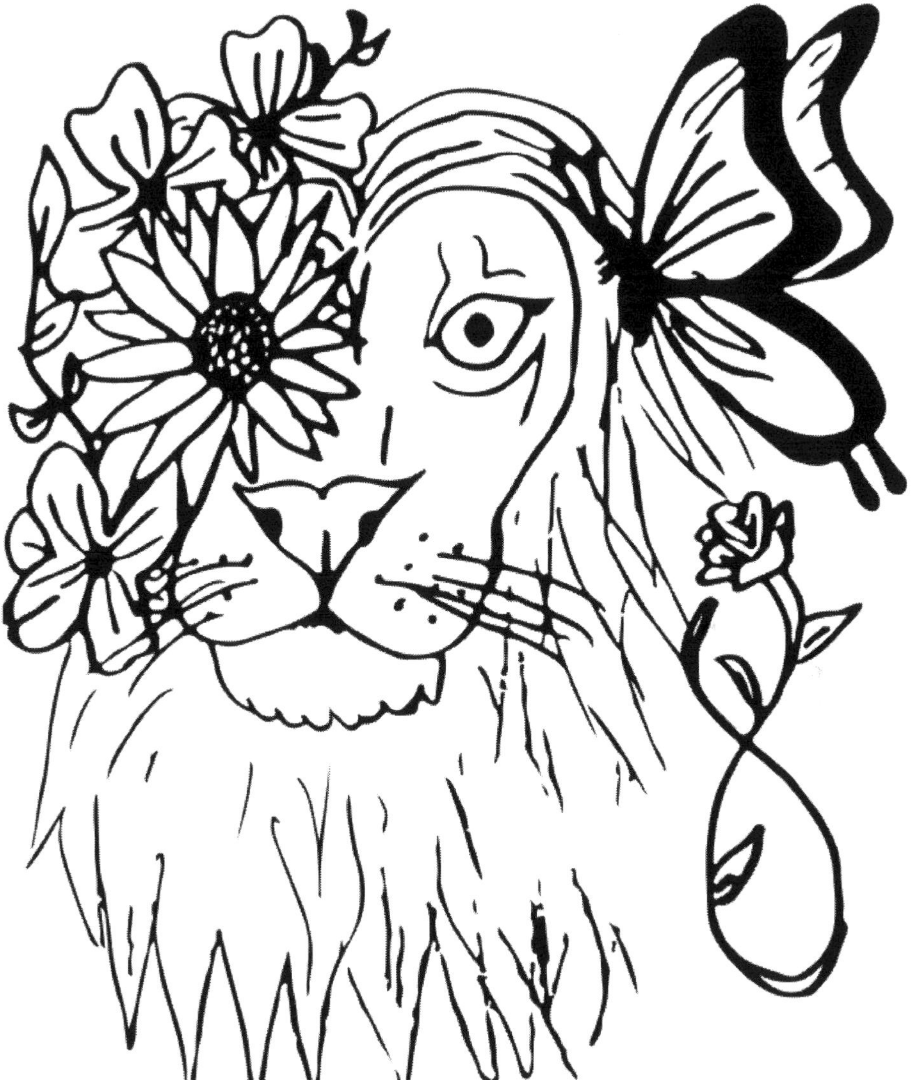

☆

Parenting your child in the stars

Wherever you are in your grief journey and no matter what you have heard, I am here to tell you that it is in fact possible to parent your child in the stars.

There are so many ways you can connect with your child, and they are there with you, every step of the way. In the raw days when Eli died I was so angry and bitter all the time, I couldn't make sense of anything and I had so many comments saying how I needed to move on. All from people who have never lost a child. I am here to tell you that I am moving on, but I am moving on with Eli. I carry him wherever I go, and despite what some people may think, I will never leave him behind.

On my hardest days when I need him the most he always shows up for me, so I make sure I show up for him too. Everything I do is for Eli, to make him proud because I'm sure that wherever he is in this universe he is patting his mama on the back, egging her on to be the best she can be.

There are many ways I connect with Eli; I meditate with some of his belongings and/or his ashes. I imagine his cheeky little face in my head. I speak to him every night when its only me awake, and I swear I can feel the love

☆

from him surrounding me. I ask him for signs all the time! Sometimes I ask for something specific, other times I ask for anything that reminds me of him, one of his songs, a lion, or Peter Pan. I ask him to visit me in ways which I associate him with such as butterflies, dragonflies, and magpies. I ask him to send me feathers and show me angel numbers. Sometimes I used to get so disappointed and disheartened when I didn't receive the signs, but I kept asking for them and eventually they came.

Just like we do, our loved ones need time to come up with a special sign for us. And I have learnt that Eli is a very, very busy little boy as he sends signs to so many people! You just have to be open with it to be able to receive them. I promise you if you allow them, they will come. All you need to do is *believe*.

Parenting our little ones looks so different to others, and so different to what we once imagined, but it's all we have. This is our mother/fatherhood and it's been different from the start! I always include Eli in everything we do because he is our son, and he always will be. Whether that's writing his name in our cards, including him in our family photos or speaking about him to our family and friends.

I have learnt throughout my grief journey that people will judge you no matter what you do, that you are grieving too much, or not enough. But I have learnt (admittedly very slowly!) that it doesn't matter what they

☆

think or how they think I 'should' be grieving, grief is different for everyone and to grieve is to love and I love Eli more and more every day, just as I would if he were here living.

That's what parents do; they love their children unconditionally. It doesn't matter if your child is heaven or earthside, we will always love them so please don't ever let anyone tell you that you can't, because I think that is impossible!

Different ways you can parent your child in the stars:

- Honour their memory, tell the world about your beautiful child. They deserve to be remembered.

- Connect with other loss parents and talk about your children together.

- Talk about your child to whoever you wish too. Don't ever let anyone make you feel bad for wanting to talk about them. You would be talking about them if they were alive, so why wouldn't you want to talk about them now.

- Develop rituals and traditions in honour of your child, such as their birthdays and anniversary dates. Honour them and celebrate your child.

- Meditation and prayer. Meditate with some of your child's belongings or their ashes if you have them, talk to them in your head. Ask them to show you love. There

☆

are lots of guided meditations on YouTube that are designed to help you to connect with your loved ones.

- Keeping their memory alive by having photos up of them or having a special place in your home dedicated to them.

- Write them a letter. Write a letter to your loved one asking questions, and a week later after meditating reply to the letter as if it was from your loved one. It may sound daft, but I really believe it worked!

- Talk to your child, ask them for specific signs. Write down any signs you may have received for them. Make sure you thank them too! Also, if you receive a sign such as a white feather or a coin, make sure you pick it up and keep it somewhere safe.

- See a medium or psychic. I have done this lots of times, and I wholeheartedly believe that they were able to connect with Eli and my loved ones. Make sure you find one with a good reputation.

Parent your child however you feel is best, however you want to, however you need to. Remember it is your child, so of course it's you that knows best. Do whatever works for you.

☆

Mindful Activities

Here are a few mindful activities that you can do as and when you wish to help ease your mind, and to focus on you. It's so important to remember to look after yourself, even though it can feel pointless to do at times it is crucial to do for your own sanity.

Meditation

Sit in a quiet space, close your eyes and focus on your breathing. Try to shut off your mind as you focus on the sensation of each inhale and exhale. You can allow thoughts to come and go, or you can use this time to connect with your child and try to communicate with them. Sometimes I sit and meditate with Eli's ashes, and it helps me to feel closer to him and connected with him.

Mindful walking

Take a slow walk outside, paying attention to each step you take and if possible your surroundings too. Feel the ground beneath your feet, and your body's movements and sensations as you walk. Really feel the sunshine or wind on your face, use this time to connect with your baby and look out for any signs they may bring you.

☆

Body Scan

Lie or sit down in a comfortable position and bring your attention to different parts of your body, starting from your toes and moving up towards your head. Notice any tension or sensations in each area. There are many YouTube videos that could help you focus on each of your body parts as you do your body scan.

Yoga

Practising Yoga can really help focus your mind, I for one struggled with this as I used to do a lot of Yoga whilst I was pregnant with Eli, so I found it to be quite triggering. I really do believe it is so helpful to our minds and our bodies though. There are also many YouTube videos if you are new to Yoga. Practise yoga poses whilst focusing on your breath and body sensations. Paying attention to the alignment of your body and the stretching of your muscles.

Mindful Eating

When in the depths of grief, some people may not eat at all whilst others use it as a coping mechanism. Today when you eat a meal or a snack notice the flavours, the textures, and aromas of the food. Chew each bite thoroughly whilst paying attention to your senses.

☆

Journaling

Writing for me was so healing in my own personal journey. Write down any thoughts and feelings that you have without any judgement. Using journalling to explore your emotions can be so healing, I used to find if I wrote down my feelings and my thoughts, it would clear my negative emotions if only for a moment. I found it so soothing to write down all my thoughts and feelings, almost if I was letting it go. I also sometimes do this and then burn the pages I've written as it felt like I was burning away the bad and negative emotions and feelings I was experiencing.

Mindful Listening

Choose a calming piece of music or nature sounds and listening attentively. Pay attention to the different instruments and sound, the rhythm, and any emotions they evoke. You could also sit outside and do this if you have a quiet space where you can sit, listen, and reflect. If you feel emotional, then really allow yourself to feel your emotions, allow yourself to cry it out if that's what your body needs to do.

Colouring or Drawing

Anything creative helped me with my healing so much, especially colouring and drawing. Sometimes I would draw or paint out my emotions or I would draw or paint a picture for Eli. If drawing isn't for you, you could use a colouring book also. Really pay attention to the colours, patterns, and movements of your hand as you colour or draw. If you are anything like me your mind may switch off for a moment or two.

Mindful Showering or Bathing

Pay attention to the sensations of the water on your skin as you bath/shower, the feeling of the soap on your skin, and the scent of the soap also. Be fully present in the experience. A freezing cold shower can also help to improve circulation, boost your immune system, reduce inflammation, and prevent muscle soreness and most important it can help to combat symptoms of depression.

You were part of me, for a little while. And even though we had to say goodbye, you will forever remain in my heart.

⭐

Brain Junk

A lot of the time I struggle to get to sleep because of the thoughts and feelings that are going round and round in my mind. Things I need to do, things I am worrying about. Just general junk. When I find I have a lot on my brain, I draw out my rubbish bin and fill it with all the junk around my head, before I try to sleep. That way I can leave it there and come back to it another day when and if I'm ready to.

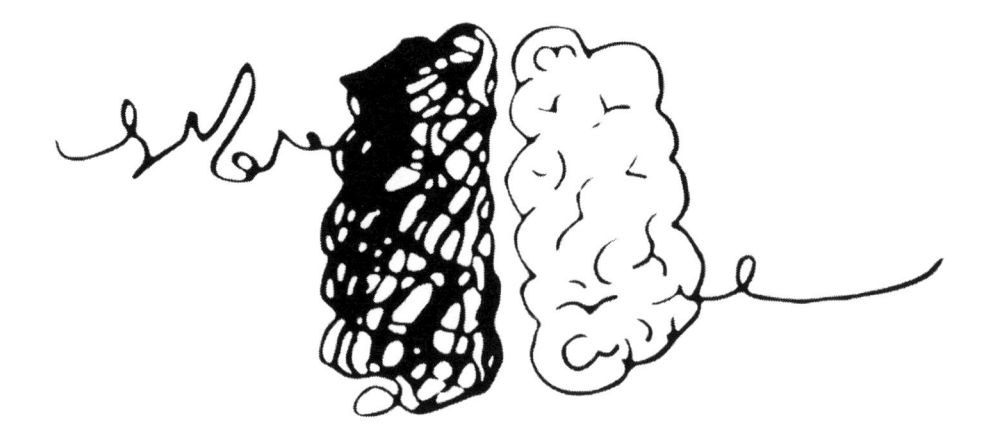

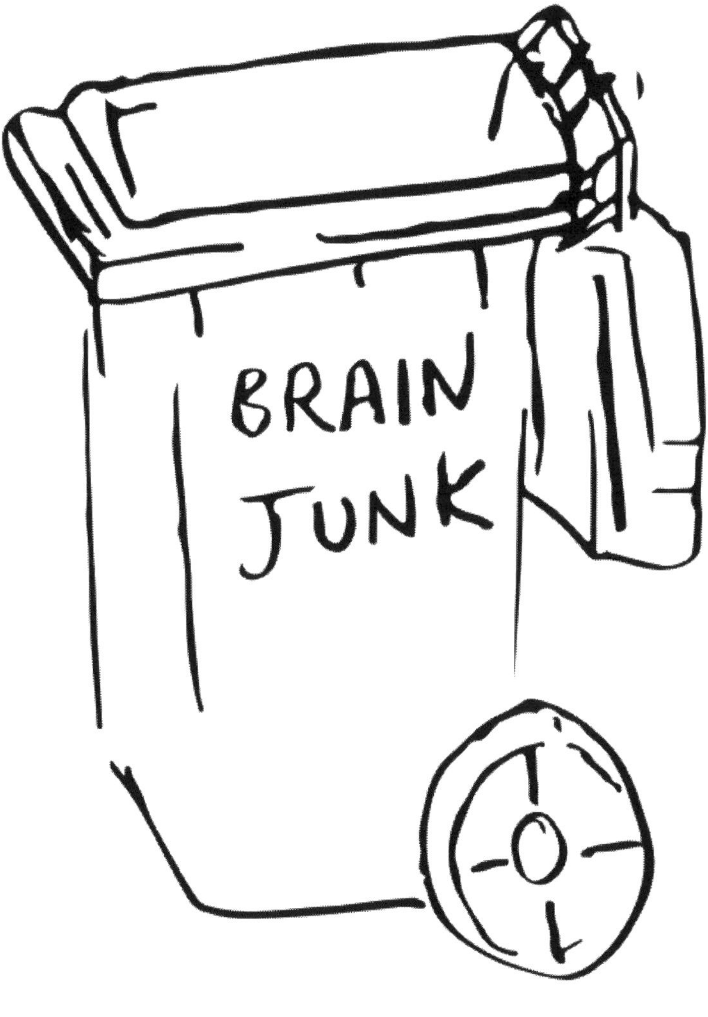
BRAIN
JUNK

☆

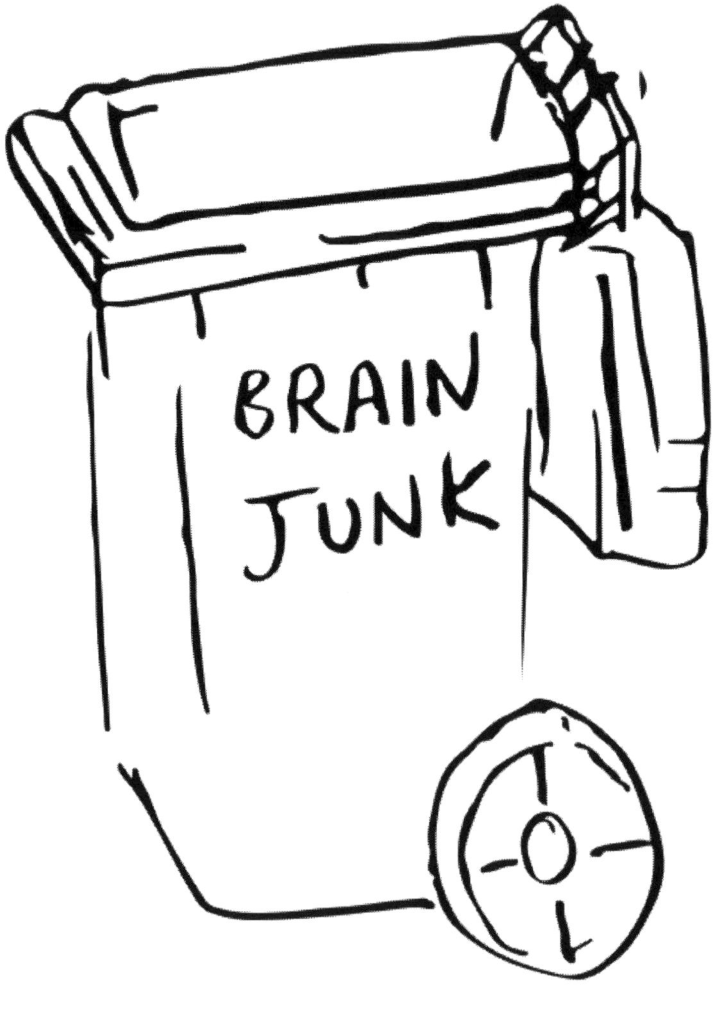
BRAIN
JUNK

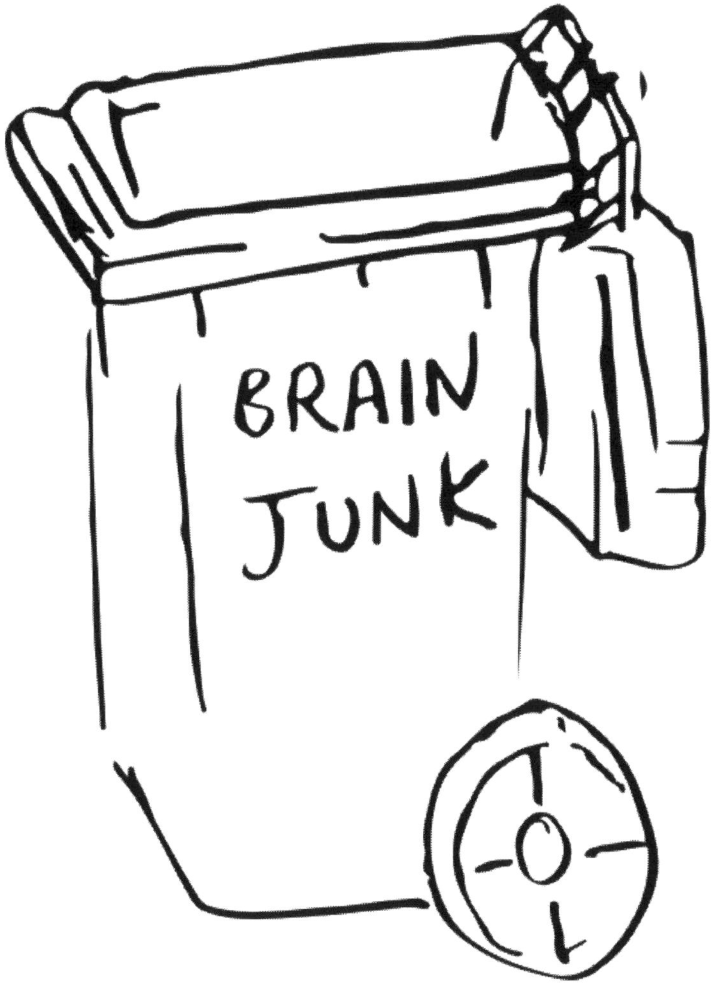
BRAIN
JUNK

☆

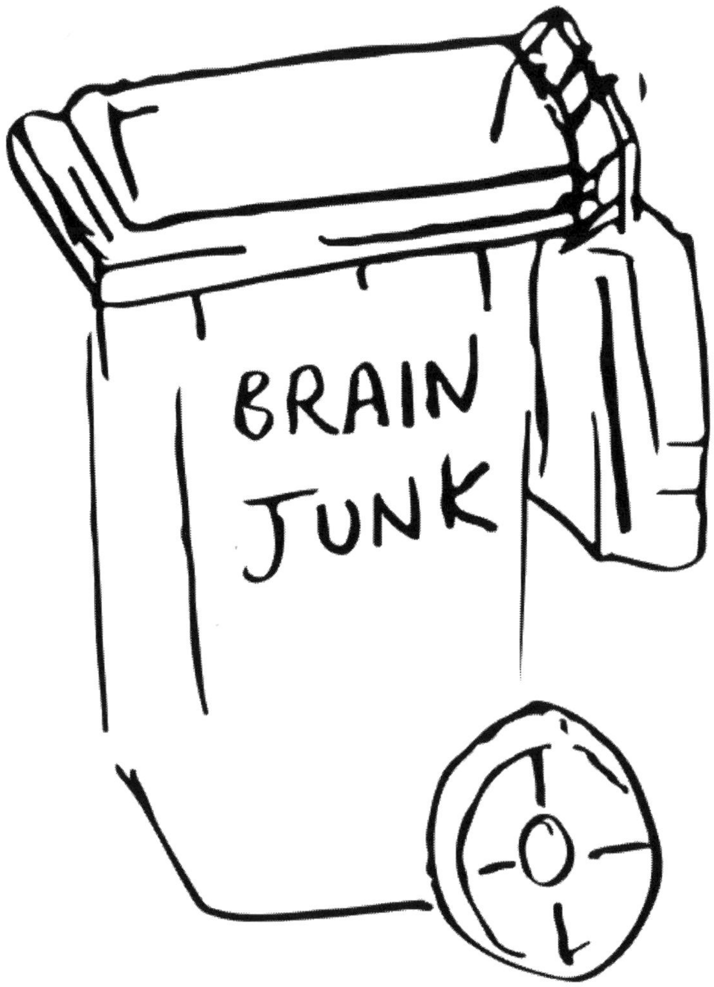
BRAIN
JUNK

Journal Prompts

I found journalling was such a healing process for me. Writing letters to Eli and talking about him through writing made my brain process what had happened and took some of the thoughts from my brain onto paper. I really hope you can find some use from these journal prompts.

I have a notebook that I write in which I imagine Eli will read. Letters to Eli telling him about how I am feeling, what has been happening lately, and how much I am missing him. For me, it's like I am spending time with Eli when I am writing to him. I feel like it's a way I can parent him without him being here to parent for physically.

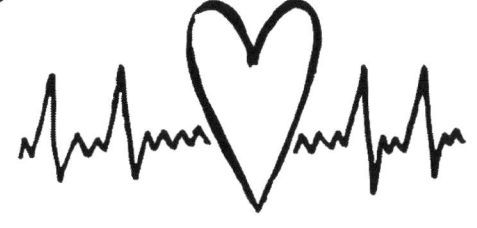

In the blink of an eye, you were gone,

Leaving us here to mourn and long.

Your time with us was much too brief,

Yet you filled our hearts with love and grief.

MY BIRTH STORY

☆

THINGS I WISH I COULD TELL MY BABY

WHAT I MISS MOST ABOUT MY BABY

☆

WHEN DO I MISS MY BABY THE MOST

☆

HOW I AM FEELING NOW

☆

THE HOPES AND DREAMS I HAD FOR MY BABY

DETAILS I WANT TO REMEMBER ABOUT MY BABY

WHAT MY PREGNANCY WAS LIKE

ALL ABOUT MY BABY

HOW I CONNECT WITH MY BABY

☆

WHO HAS BEEN MY BIGGEST SUPPORT

A LETTER TO MY PARTNER

☆

A LETTER TO MYSELF

A LETTER TO MY BABY

☆

☆

☆

Getting Our Rainbow

Dakota-Rose Eli Tookey was born on the 16th July 2023. I was induced when I was 38 weeks pregnant, simply because 1. I was an anxious mess and wasn't coping at all and 2. Her movements had reduced just like Eli's did.

I could write a whole other book on pregnancy after loss and parenting after loss. When I was pregnant with her my emotions were all over the place, I was disassociated with my pregnancy and filled with feelings of guilt, dread, and anxiety, I was adamant I wouldn't be bringing her home either. I couldn't buy her anything at all in case I tempted fate. Luckily our parents had been buying her clothes and things otherwise she would have had nothing when she was born, of course we still had Eli's stuff but most of it was packed away somewhere.

I still don't know how I got through those 8.5 months when I was pregnant with her but somehow I did and I'm watching my beautiful rainbow daughter sleeping in her cot right now. I still can't believe she is here. Although parenting after loss is a whole different range of emotions too. I am still filled with anxiety and can't have her sleep without her sock that measures her heart rate and oxygen levels. There is always that fear that somehow she will also be taken from me. But I am trying my hardest every day to fight my anxieties and just be in the present moment with her.

I'm so grateful that I am able to watch her grow and meet new milestones every day. It is something I will never take for granted. All the while being even more aware of what I have missed out on with Eli these past two years and wondering even more what he would be like now. Grief now is a whole new different experience for me, and it's a new kind of grief wave I'm experiencing.

When we are out with her we are constantly being asked if she is our first child or how many children we have, and we always get the same disappointing and awkward reactions from others and honestly I find it draining. If only baby loss wasn't such a taboo then perhaps people would react differently.

I will never deny his existence despite other people's reactions, we will always be a family of four, even though others only see the three of us. I am so proud of my Son, and I love talking about him any chance I am given.

Dakota has taught me that there is hope after the storm, but I do not see Eli as the storm, the pain of losing him is. Dakota has taught me that joy and grief can coexist, and she has taught me to love again and to love myself again. To appreciate myself and my body knowing that I was able to get her here safely. She is also exclusively breastfed, so I am also so proud of my body for continuing to help her grow and thrive.

Pregnancy after loss was me facing all my trauma again, and honestly it was awful. But I am so proud of myself for persevering in getting pregnant, and fighting until the end despite the PTSD and all the flashbacks I was having.

Surprisingly Dakota was the most relaxed new-born baby I've ever met, and she slept so much in her first month she was born, hence my reduced movements with her. She is just so chilled I always joke about how on earth I created such a chilled-out baby when I was so anxious, stressed, and fearful when carrying her. I felt so guilty for Eli when I was pregnant, but also so guilty for her for feeling like I couldn't connect with her, but really I was only trying to protect myself and my heart from more pain.

I was so scared I didn't love her as much as I should have but I loved her more than anything already, and that is why I was so fearful of something going wrong again. All the worries melted away when I was able to hold her for the first time, I still couldn't believe we did it. Everything was all so surreal, especially that journey home from the hospital with her. Surreal but sad that we should have done the same with Eli too. We were crying

☆

happy and sad tears on that journey home and played Eli's songs to Dakota for the first time.

Parenting after loss is also like being divided in two, parenting one child earthside and one child in heaven comes with lots of emotions. It is constantly feeling bad and worrying that Eli will be forgotten about and that I'm not doing enough for his memory anymore, because I'm too busy caring for his little sister. Of course I am just doing the best I can to make sure I am there for both of my children, and I am sure I would feel similar emotions and guilt if he was here with us earthside as my time would still have to be divided between them both.

Dakota really is the most amazing human with the most amazing soul, we know for sure that Eli brought her to us to help us to heal our hearts. She certainly brings us so much joy on the darkest of days and we will continue to do the best we can to make sure she has the best childhood possible. We are so thankful and grateful for her and to Eli for bringing her to us. We know he is the best big brother to her; we talk about him all the time still and we will continue to do so. Dakota will learn all about her amazing big brother when she's old enough to understand, and I will make sure that she deals with others grief and sadness with compassion and sympathy.

Thank you Dakota for being the best daughter we could ask for and for bringing us so much love and joy every single day, you really are such a blessing to us and the

⭐

perfect addition to our little family. We will forever be grateful to have you and to watch you grow, little one.

When I was pregnant with Dakota I kept seeing butterflies all the time, everywhere I went and I'm sure it was Eli sending us signs and giving us hope when we needed it the most.

Dakota-Rose our beautiful little butterfly.

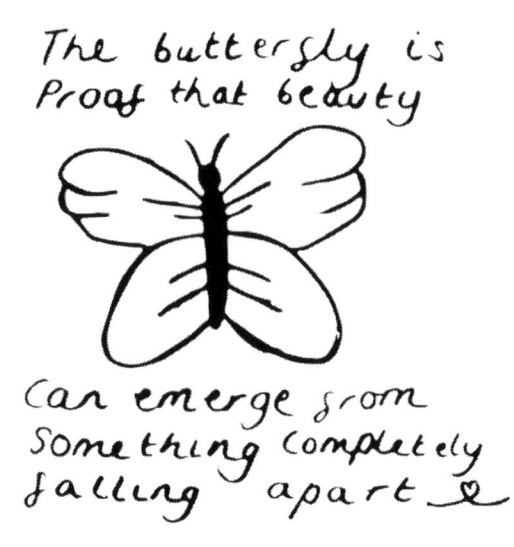

The butterfly is proof that beauty can emerge from something completely falling apart ♡

Butterflies symbolise a deep and powerful representation of life, they mirror transformation and rebirth. They are beautiful and have mystery, symbolism, and meaning.

In many spiritual traditions, butterflies are also symbols of the soul and its journey. Their delicate beauty and ephemeral nature remind us of the fleeting, precious nature of life and the importance of embracing change with hope and grace.

They can be seen as messengers of transformation, encouraging us to embrace the unknown and trust in the process of evolution.

Help & Support

Sands

(Stillbirth and Neonatal Death Society) is a UK wide charity that offers support to anyone affected by the death of a baby. They provide helpline services, local support groups, online forums, and resources for bereaved parents and healthcare professionals.

www.sands.org.uk

Tommys

Tommys is a charity that funds research into the causes and prevention of miscarriage, stillbirth and premature birth. They provide support and information to parents who have experienced baby loss, including a helpline, online support and local support groups.

www.tommys.org

The Miscarriage Association

This charity provides support and information to individuals and couples who have experienced pregnancy loss, including miscarriage, ectopic pregnancy, and molar pregnancy. They offer a helpline, online support forums, and resources for healthcare professionals.

www.miscarraigeassociation.org.uk

Aching Arms

Aching Arms is a charity that provides comfort bears to families who have experienced baby loss. These bears are given as a symbol of remembrance and support. The charity also offers online support and resources for bereaved parents.

www.achingarms.co.uk

Petals

Petals is a charity that offers specialised counselling and support for individuals and couples who have experienced baby loss during pregnancy or shortly after birth. They provide face-to-face counselling in certain locations and online counselling for those unable to access in-person support.

www.petalscharity.org

Saying Goodbye

Saying Goodbye provides support and services for those who have suffered the loss of a baby at any stage of pregnancy, birth, or in infancy. They offer remembrance services, support groups, and online resources for bereaved parents and families.

www.sayinggoodbye.org

Lennys Legacy

Lenny's legacy is a registered charity, (1201987) which aims to support parents bereaved through all forms of pregnancy, infant and child loss. The organisation was founded by bereaved parents Roy and Mim in memory of their two sons, Lenny and Bhai who tragically died.

Lenny's legacy organises regular and one off events for bereaved parents and their families. Face to face events are in Sheffield and the surrounding area but they also offer a number of online events.

Their website has usable, bite-sized information on various topics to support parents.

Additionally, the charity has a focus on, "supporting the supporters." They do this by providing accessible, online resources tailored to different audiences such as friends, family and professionals.

Lenny's legacy also provides high quality professional training for healthcare professionals, lawyers and employers - the training combines personal stories and practical tools and is informed by theory and research.

www.lennyslegacy.co.uk

Measure the Placenta

Measure the Placenta support measurement of the placenta using Estimated Placental Volume (EPV) as a standard practice of prenatal care. They aim to help families seeking answers, to supply the medical community with an archive of published research linking small placentas to poor outcomes, to inform doctors, nurses, doulas and ultrasound technicians of the availability of EPV to potentially save lives, and to drive attention and awareness to close the gap in care.

www.measuretheplacenta.org

Kicks Count

Kicks Count aims to reduce the UK's high stillbirth and neonatal death rate by raising awareness of baby movements.

While there isn't one cause of stillbirth, a decrease in baby's movements can be a key warning sign that a baby is in distress and 50% of mothers who had a stillbirth noticed slowing down of baby's movements beforehand.

By raising awareness of baby's movements and encouraging mums to report any change in movement immediately it is estimated that a third of stillbirths could be prevented.

www.kickscount.org.uk

☆

A big thank you to everyone who has supported me throughout this journey. Especially my husband Dean and our wonderful parents. Thank you to everyone who continues to love, include and remember our son. Thank you to the loss mama community who continue to support me and remember Eli. Also, a big thank you to David Cunningham for all the help and support in creating this book and making it possible for me to do so. And most of all a big thank you to Eli, for giving me his strength and for encouraging me to be a better person, and a better mother. I love you.

Connect with me further on Instagram @rememberingeli @chelseytookey

Listen to my podcast below, hosted with another loss mum. Where we offer comfort, connection and remembrance for families navigating the pain of baby loss.

"Remember Me - The Stories of Our Babies"

out now on Spotify, Amazon Music & Apple Music.

I'll hold you in my heart until I hold you in Heaven.

Printed in Great Britain
by Amazon

296b4659-88ee-45da-91fe-d7b0918676baR01